Dear Becky,

This book opened my eyes and heart as to "why" people make certain choices. And, "why" I react so strongly to certain situations. I found it to be very affirming!

Enjoy retirement girlfriend ♥ You go into the broken places of the world now. Think what is ahead of you!!!

Love & Joy to you—

Eyes on Home, Jan

What People Are Saying about *A Why to Live For*

"Do you want to do something significant for God in a way that resonates with who you are, and with your unique passions? Then here's a truly remarkable book that will help you define what God's mission for your life is, and do so in a practical, personal, easy-to-access way.

Dave Rod's brilliant and insightful book is not a book to read at one sitting. I found myself reaching for my pen and journal with the reading of each chapter, eager to process and pray for God's prompting and direction. This is mission made accessible in a way where each one of us is deeply gripped by our unique makeup and what the 'good works that God prepared for us in advance' are.

Read it at your own joyous peril. It will change you."
—Bishop Oscar Muriu
Nairobi Chapel, Nairobi, Kenya

"When we come to grips with the fact that we truly are God's masterpiece, our world turns upside down. If we move into Kingdom living, we begin to intersect with the world's brokenness and discover our unique calling. But when we embark on this journey, we might just discover we've been asking the wrong questions all along. In A Why to Live For, Dave Rodriguez challenges us with a whole new set of questions."
—Anita Lustrea
Host of Faith Conversations podcast
spiritual director, author,
media coach

"There are so many people going to church and reading their Bibles who know that God is calling them to something more, but don't have any idea where to start. If I could put one book in their hands, it would be A Why to Live For. *This book is honest, practical, and inspirational. There's no getting around the fact that we live in a broken world; this book artfully dismantles any excuse we might have for not doing anything about it."*

—Josiah Haken
VP, Outreach Operations
New York City Relief

"Books like this make me revisit my dismissal of religion and proudly proclaim a faith in the face of popular secularism. If Dave is not right in his view of God's Kingdom and our enthralling place in His plan, it's not a life that interests me all that much."

—David C. Baker
author of *The Business of Expertise*
and termed "the expert's expert" by the *New York Times*

"A Why to Live For is well written and researched. It is conversational yet substantial. Dave's pastoral and practical voice comes through, as well as his love for scripture. But, what is startling is that he manages to do all of this without employing platitudes, threats, or coercion. This book is pastoral and prophetic, humane and activistic."*

—Jim Henderson, D Min
author of *Jim and Casper Go to Church*
executive producer of Jim Henderson Presents

"Senior Pastor Dave Rodriguez is a passionate man. A Why to Live For *not only captures the author's passion for Christ but provides a serious engagement of Jesus' proclamation that the Kingdom of God has arrived. This book is no leisurely read about the Kingdom of God, but rather a robust call to Kingdom living. More specifically, this book is an invitation to know and live your God-given destiny! When Kingdom of God consciousness grips the soul, enabling us to identify our gifts and calling in light of the world's real needs, we discover* A Why to Live For.

Take note: the author is not writing vague generalities but identifies and explores six specific callings. Each of these callings are ways by which we live out Kingdom of God realities and we come to grasp our destiny in Christ. The author, with classic pastoral teaching, leads the reader to a rich understanding of each calling through life stories of real people. He provides suggested ways the reader can begin to live their personal destiny. This book challenges the very fiber of a contemporary Christianity formed in a culture of narcissistic indulgence and entitlement. This book is gritty, provoking, and inviting. It echoes the words of the Apostle James, 'Faith without works is dead.' This is a book for pastors, elders, deacons, trustees, and every serious-minded believer who follows Jesus. This is also a book for the confused, the perplexed, the ambivalent, the skeptical, and even the cynical. Read this book and share it with others. It will transform your life and theirs!"

—Rich Plass, PhD
founder and executive director of CrossPoint Ministry

"Author, pastor, and friend, Dave Rodriguez, provides us a holistic view of the challenges Christians face in answering Jesus' prayer, 'Thy Kingdom come, Thy will be done, on Earth

as it is in Heaven.' Through his dissection of the broken places of society and his highlighting of the Kingdom's solution, Rodriguez provides clear direction on how to engage in building the Kingdom today. This is a guide to bringing relevance to the Church in a broken world."

—Rev. Jay Height
executive director
Shepherd Community Center
Indianapolis, IN

"A Why to Live For *is a compelling and motivating book that will have big impact on you from its very first pages. This the message the Church needs to hear—powerful, inspirational! It will surely reignite your passion for the Kingdom and may just be the tool you need to help you find your calling."*
—Ira Venglovska
director, Mission to Ukraine

"A timely, must-read *for those aspiring to be purpose-driven leaders! Our world is crying out for more leaders and organizations that are unleashed and chasing a greater purpose. There is no bigger WHY than the 6 Broken Places of the world.*

Pastor, prophet, and purpose-driven leader . . . that is what you have in Dave Rodriguez. You get to ride along and experience his four decades of humble, courageous leadership through stories, principles, and practices that are catalyzing churches, communities, and companies to engage the 6 Broken Places of the world. His life mission has moved thousands into the ultimate WHY of chasing a bigger calling.

My hope is that this book starts a greater movement to better the world through inspired purpose-driven leadership!
—Jeff Simmons
president and CEO, Elanco Animal Health

A WHY TO LIVE FOR

*Where Your Destiny Meets
the Broken Places of the World*

Dave Rodriguez

N|T NEWTYPE

Editing by Cara Highsmith, Highsmith Creative Services, www. highsmithcreative.com

Cover and Interior Design by Mitchell Shea

Printed in the United States of America

First Edition 14 13 12 11 10 / 10 9 8 7 6 5 4 3 2 1

DEDICATION

To Penny, my love and my dearest friend, without whom I would not know beauty and without whom I would never find my destiny.

ACKNOWLEDGEMENTS

I'm so grateful for the many people who have helped bring this book to completion! Not only have you provided your skills, but also your heart and encouragement!

Thank you to . . .

Cara, for your wonderful assistance, direction, and editing in the formation of this book!

Penny, for your painstaking detailed editing of all my commas and other grammatical faux pas!

Kathy, for the patient transcription!

Mitch Shea, for your outstanding design work!

Ron and Meg, for the place of respite and inspiration to write!

Tim and Barry, for the sermon material and insights!

The pastors, staff, and people of Grace Church, for sharing in the story behind the book!

And the family: Penny, Barry, Liv, Lucy, Kevin, Vic, Chris, Isa, Anya, and Jude, for the hugs and cheers to keep on going!

CONTENTS

Introduction I

Chapter 1 - You 1

Chapter 2 - The Champion 7

Chapter 3 - Nurturers 39

Chapter 4 - Healers 73

Chapter 5 - Stewards 99

Chapter 6 - Activists 125

Chapter 7 - Ambassadors 159

Chapter 8 - Finding Your Destiny 187

Afterword 201

About Dave 203

Notes 205

FOREWORD

The best sound is one that cannot be ignored. Picture a busy city street where no one is talking to each other and they are each lost in their own lives, sitting, walking, and running. They are in orbits that don't intersect. Then this lively tune, full of hope and life, seems to rise from nowhere. It catches them off guard as they look at each other for clues. The melody takes shape and the individuals become a movement, suddenly, united by a common longing. That is what this book does.

—David C. Baker
author of *The Business of Expertise* and termed "the expert's expert" by the *NY Times*

A WHY TO LIVE FOR

Dave Rodriguez

INTRODUCTION

In 1991 we founded Grace Church. It grew quickly, expanding beyond our capacity to figure things out. All along I had felt somewhat ill-prepared to lead such an organization. Mostly, I just did the next thing necessary and tried to direct us to do what the church is supposed to do . . . or what I thought the church was supposed to do. Truth be told, I was kinda lost. I knew people were looking for a clear call to action but wasn't sure how to form a coherent, compelling, or sticky vision. So, I read (and prayed, of course). I read pretty much everything I could get my hands on about leadership in the local church.

Along the way, I discovered something that was news to me, yet was a concept that had been under my nose for as long as I had been reading the Bible—something I had studied in my college Bible school education but never understood, or, more to the point, had *mis*understood. It was the idea of the Kingdom of God . . . make that the *revolutionary* idea of the Kingdom of God.

Really, the concept is hard to miss, especially in the gospels, as Jesus referred to it again and again:

> Jesus went into Galilee, where he preached God's Good News. "The time promised by God has come at last!" he announced. "The Kingdom of God is near! Repent of your sins and believe the Good News!"
>
> —Mark 1:14-15

and...

Soon afterward Jesus began a tour of the
nearby towns and villages, preaching and
announcing the Good News about the Kingdom
of God.

—Luke 8:1

But, for years I had mistakenly (or ignorantly) simply equated the Kingdom of God with Heaven itself, something to be enjoyed post-mortem in Paradise. Or else, I spiritualized it as some kind of metaphor of my own soul before God. Or, I shoved it way out into some future reality after Jesus had returned, cleaned shop, and permanently installed this kingdom on a re-created planet. I honestly never considered that the Kingdom of God could be . . . would be . . . here and now—a clear and present reality introduced by Jesus himself, the reign of God, not delayed, and not in part, fully available and graspable right at this very moment!

Several authors woke me up to the near and present Kingdom of God, but none more effectively than the late Dallas Willard. Willard, through his book, *The Divine Conspiracy*, opened a doorway into a new world of mission and vision and purpose. He absolutely captivated me with his exposition and explanation of the Kingdom of God. Here are just a few of the ways he described the Kingdom of God:

- The Kingdom of God is "the rule of God, now present in the person of Jesus himself. It is God's program for human history."

- The Kingdom of God is "not something confined to the inner world of human consciousness. It is not some matter of inner attitude or faith that might be totally disconnected from the public, behavioral, visible world. It always pervades and governs the whole of the physical universe. When Jesus directs us to pray 'thy kingdom come,' he does not mean that we should pray for it to come into existence. Rather we pray for it to take over at all points in the personal, social, and political order where it is not excluded."[1]

Many other authors have contributed to my deepening understanding of God's Kingdom as well. Here is just a sampling of the awesome and inspiring definitions I've come across:

- Daryl Guder in his book *The Missional Church*, describes the Kingdom as "God's demanding care and compassionate rule . . . a social world full of peace grounded in justice."[2]

- Brian McLaren says it is "a political, social, religious, artistic, economic, intellectual and spiritual revolution that would give birth to a new world order that will overthrow the status quo in nearly every conceivable way."[3]

- Donald Kraybill pictures God's reign as an inverted, or upside-down way of life that contrasts with the prevailing world order.[4]

- N.T. Wright declares that the Kingdom is the sovereign rule of God . . . breaking in to the present world.[5]

And finally, Christopher Wright, in his incredible exposition of the Mission of God, gives a full picture of God's Kingdom—God's rule—in all its glory:

> The reign of (God), when it would finally come, would mean justice for the oppressed and overthrow of the wicked. It would bring true peace to the nations and the abolition of war, and training for war. It would put an end to poverty, want and need, and provide everyone with economic viability. It would mean a satisfying and fulfilling life for human families, safety for children, and fulfillment for the elderly, without danger from enemies, and all of this within a renewed creation free from harm and threat. It would mean the inversion of the moral values that dominate the current world order, for in the Kingdom of God the upside-down priorities of the beatitudes operate.[6]

As I read Willard's and the others' eye-opening explanations of the Kingdom, I was stunned. How on earth had I missed this? I had read and re-read these words of Jesus:

> "The time promised by God has come at last!"
> he announced. "The Kingdom of God is near!
> Repent of your sins and believe the Good
> News!"
>
> —Mark 1:15

I realized I had totally skimmed over the word "near" (which means immediate imminence). I had pushed the marvelous reign of God out to some indeterminate future. I had labored under the impression that the good news of the Kingdom was limited simply to personal salvation through faith in Jesus. I also perceived that I had limited the good news of the Kingdom to the joy of going to Heaven after you die, and thus did not see any of its social, physical, psychological, and relational transformation possibilities in this very life. What a revelation this all was to me! And an embarrassment.

Once past this awakening, I started to turn my attention to practical matters of application, especially for my church. What did it all mean? How do we grasp it? What does it mean to pray for the Kingdom of God to come?

> Pray like this: Our Father in Heaven, may your name be kept holy. May your Kingdom come soon.
> —Matthew 6:9

And what did it mean for the church to be given the keys of the Kingdom? How could those keys, presumably, unlock the power of the Kingdom?

> I say to you that . . . upon this rock I will build my church, and all the powers of hell will not conquer it. And I will give you the keys of the Kingdom of Heaven.
> —Matthew 16:18-19

And if the Kingdom of God is present, then how would we know? What are its signs and indications? If God was ruling or reigning at a particular moment in history at a specific place on the planet, how would we know?

In short . . . **What are the evidences of the Kingdom of God?**

I studied the Scriptures; I accumulated; I categorized and sorted. Here's what I came up with:

6 Evidences of the Kingdom of God:

1. **Reconciliation with God** – Where the Kingdom of God is evident, you'll find human beings who have repented, been forgiven, and adopted as children of God through faith in Jesus Christ.

2. **Community and loving relationships among human beings** – Where the Kingdom of God is evident, you'll find people, once alone and isolated, now discovering relationship, mercy, and love in community with others.

3. **Healing of minds, bodies, and spirits** – Where the Kingdom of God is evident you'll discover physical, psychological, and relational wellness being restored and pain being healed.

4. **Peace** - Where the Kingdom of God is evident, you'll notice people from diverse ethnicities, nations, and people groups living and loving in community. And you'll experience the end of hatred, racism, discrimination, bigotry, prejudice, and intolerance.

5. **A restored and beautiful physical planet** – Where the Kingdom of God is evident, you'll observe the planet itself being cared for—the decay of God's "very good" world halted.

6. **Justice** – Where the Kingdom of God is evident, you'll rejoice over seeing vast systems of human poverty, misery, and brokenness coming to an end.

Over several years, I introduced these concepts of the Kingdom of God and described these evidences to our congregation. As I taught the Kingdom and thought the Kingdom and discussed the Kingdom and all its evidences, I slowly began to reimagine our church and its purpose in the world. Like all organizations, we had a purpose statement that defined us. We said that we existed "to make disciples of Jesus Christ and launch them into the mission of God." But, now newly armed with a better idea of what God wanted us to be about, we began to reshape what we meant by those key words "disciples of Jesus" and "mission of God."

Lightbulbs went off in our heads as we started asking: "If these are the 6 Evidences of the Kingdom of God, then what kind of people or disciples of Jesus are we trying to create? If Jesus sent his followers out with the charge to declare that the Kingdom of God had come, then that would mean those same followers should be people who encouraged reconciliation with God, offered love to isolated people, prayed for healing everywhere they went, sought to bring people together regardless of ethnicity or nationality, cared for the planet, and became ministers of justice wherever they lived.

I started to quote Tom Sine frequently, who reminded us that we have no right to "wait for soul rescue while living for fat city." We've got a job to do! We have the authority of God behind us and the keys to the Kingdom in our pocket.

I tried to express, albeit less poetically than N.T. Wright, the responsibility that was ours to advance the Kingdom:

You are not oiling the wheels of a machine that's about to roll over a cliff. You are not restoring a great painting that's shortly going to be thrown on the fire. You are not planting roses in a garden that's about to be dug up for a building site. You are – strange though it may seem – accomplishing something that will become in due course part of God's new world. Every act of love, gratitude and kindness; every minute spent teaching a severely handicapped child to read or to walk; every act of care and nurture, of comfort and support for one's fellow human beings and for that matter one's fellow non-human creatures; and, of course, every deed that spreads the gospel, builds up the church, embraces and embodies holiness rather than corruption, and makes the name of Jesus honored in the world – all of this will find its way, through the resurrecting power of God, into the new creation...[7]

I tried to help our people understand that God's mission was our mission. I began to describe the Kingdom and its evidences as "what gets God out of bed in the morning." These six tasks are on his daily to-do list. These are God's personal goals! Our people started to get it . . . mostly. Many times, I got blank looks from people. The idea of "Kingdom" is certainly not a concept 21st century folks grasp readily.

Then one day, in the late 90s, while sitting on my back deck with Tim Ayers, our teaching pastor, we had a burst of insight. We had been concerned that the 6 Evidences of the Kingdom weren't sticky enough to be remembered or embraced.

They really weren't. And it frustrated us.

So, in our musings about it, we flipped the coin to the other side, so to speak, and started playing around with an idea: if these are the *evidences* of the kingdom, then what does it look like when they are *not present*? The "6 Broken Places" came to us so quickly we could hardly write them down fast enough. And when we began to teach them, to emphasize them, and to construct ministry around them we realized how truly sticky they were. Today, people at Grace Church may not remember all of them, but they'll get most of them right, most of the time.

The 6 Broken Places stuck.

Now, watch how this plays out as I put the 6 Evidences of the Kingdom side by side with their counterparts, the 6 Broken Places:

The 6 Evidences of the Kingdom of God	The 6 Broken Places
Reconciliation with God	Separation
Love and community among human beings	Isolation
Healing of minds, bodies, and spirits	Pain
Peace among diverse ethnicities and people groups	Hatred
A restored and beautiful physical planet	Decay
Justice	Injustice

Here, then, is a short synopsis of each of the 6 Broken Places:

SEPARATION:
Since the moment humanity began to rebel against God under the lying influence of Satan, the world has been broken. First and foremost, humanity now experiences SEPARATION *from God*. Having "fallen short of his glory," we live in an unreconciled state with him. We are lost, without hope or a future.

ISOLATION:
Human beings live in ISOLATION from one another. Real community is vanishing, and loneliness is commonplace.

PAIN:
Our bodies and minds are overwhelmed with PAIN. This pain is physical, emotional, and mental, and its source is everything from cancer to depression to heartbreak.

HATRED:
We have become increasingly filled with HATRED toward one another. Racism, ethnic conflict, ideological antagonism, and unfiltered fury are all too common in our world.

DECAY:
The physical creation, itself, has been experiencing DECAY. God's "very good" creation groans under neglect and abuse.

INJUSTICE:
Nearly everywhere, vast systems of wrong and INJUSTICE have been perpetuated for millennia. Soul-crushing poverty, life-ending abortion, food insecurity, and human trafficking, to name just a few, are tragic day-to-day realities in our world.

And, there you have it. The 6 Broken Places. The 6 states of the human condition where the Kingdom is not fulfilling its promise, and where we are being called to accomplish "something that will become, in due course, part of God's new world." The world is broken. Even if you are a "glass half full" kind of person you know that is a fair assessment. The world is in deep, deep agony and we all feel it; do we not? We sigh, ball up our fists, and throw our hands up in frustration as we observe the mess around us . . .

. . . as we stare down the red-faced fury of racism;

. . . as we read of another boatload of refugees drowning in the Mediterranean;

. . . as we watch the planet decay before our very eyes;

. . . as we hear of yet another person who has taken their own life out of sheer loneliness and depression;

. . . as we stand bedside with a friend immobilized with some horrific disease;

. . . as we cry ourselves to sleep over our child who has turned his back on God;

. . . as we face poverty, and abortion, and genocide, and human trafficking, and, and, and . . .

I am sickened just thinking about this stuff. And at the same time, I find myself, once again, angry and worked up . . . anxious to do something . . . anything . . . to end this litany of dismay!

But, what do they have to do with you?

Let me show you.

CHAPTER 1
YOU

*"We were built to count, as water is made to run downhill.
We are placed in a specific context to count in ways no one
else does. That is our destiny."*
—Dallas Willard, Divine Conspiracy

Before you were born, before you took on form, God looked at you and was pleased. Quite pleased. He not only loved you (which you've been told from your childhood by pastors and parents), but he *liked* you! He liked how he made you, how he designed you, and how he equipped you. He liked your latent personality and your skill set. He liked your body type (yes, he did). He liked your mind, your heart, and your spunk. He liked your grit and your passion.

Yeah, he was quite pleased with you. He did a very good job making you, didn't he? As a matter of fact, he was so tickled with how you turned out . . . or, rather, how you were about to turn out, that without hesitation he labeled you a masterpiece!

A masterpiece . . . you.

You made all the delicate, inner parts of my body
and knit me together in my mother's womb.
Thank you for making me so wonderfully complex!
Your workmanship is marvelous—how well I know it.

You watched me as I was being formed in utter seclusion,
as I was woven together in the dark of the womb.
You saw me before I was born.
Every day of my life was recorded in your book.
Every moment was laid out
before a single day had passed.

—Psalm 139:13-16

David, the psalm writer, realized that he was made . . . don't miss this . . . wonderfully and marvelously! So incredible was he that it freaked him out a bit. "Fearfully made" is how he originally described himself.

This is you too! And this is very important. Hugely important. Massively important. Not just to make you feel better. Not just to perk you up. Not just to give you a little pat on the back. Not just for an "at a boy" or "at a girl."

No. It is so significant that you grasp your identity as a masterpiece, so crucial that you come to grips with your God-created capacities, so vital that you accept your uniqueness because the fate of the world hangs in the balance. The world is groaning in anticipation and in hope that you will get your stuff together, love who God made you to be, roll up your sleeves, get to work, and find your destiny.

Here it is in one bold statement: "For we are God's masterpiece, created in Christ Jesus to do good works, which God prepared in advance for us to do." (Ephesians 2:10)

Masterpiece . . . that's you, but made that way—deeply liked and deeply loved—for a reason. To do good works—occupations or labors that are intrinsically good. Efforts that are, by their nature, good because they are things that: 1) God thinks are good, and 2) God chose for you to do way in advance

. . . as in, before you were born. Works that feed the world's great hunger. Works that address the world's great groaning. Works that heal the brokenness of humanity and the planet. Works that repair the 6 Broken Places of the World!

This book is about those works. But, really, at the end of the day, it's about you. I believe deeply that you have within you a capacity that few others have to heal one of those confounded broken places of the world . . . or two . . . or more.

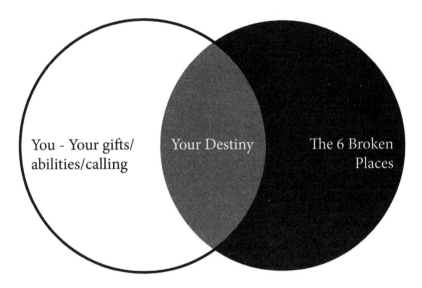

I hope this diagram will give you a clearer picture of how this principle shows up in your life. The left circle represents you with your unique capacities, personality, gifts, abilities, desires, and calling. The right circle represents the 6 Broken Places of the World. Where the two intersect is the place where your unique design and deep desires meet the broken places. It is your Ephesians 2:10 destiny! It is where you will find your greatest joy, fulfillment, and meaning. It is where a spark will be lit within you, your passion ignited.

But, you may be wondering, *Does everyone have one? Why does it matter? How do I know what my calling is?* First, I will say, yes, I believe everyone has a calling or purpose. We all have a reason we were put here and a role to step into. Discovering, embracing, and fulfilling your calling matters, because our individual callings all fit together in an incredible mosaic, and as Ephesians 2:10 tells us, we were made to do the work of God while we are here. The work we are designated to do is important to that larger work and plan God has set in motion. Finally, identifying your calling is a process, and I believe we have different callings at different points in our lives that change based on the skills, experiences, and gifts we accumulate and cultivate, and they all come together to form your ultimate destiny. In the last chapter of the book I will give you a tool that will help you zero in on your destiny; but, for now, what you need to know is that you discover your calling by being intentional about looking at what lights your fire, what you care about most, and finding where your skills, abilities, and gifts might meet a need, eradicate a problem, or make something better.

This stuff is so potent, so motivating, so compelling that, within moments of describing the concept, I find people leaning way over the table, hanging on every word, and in many cases weeping as the lightbulb goes on for them. Such is the captivating power of calling and destiny. I've watched tears stream down the cheeks of corporate executives, politicians, professional athletes, pastors, teachers, farmers, and tradesmen, not to mention hundreds of students just beginning their quest, as they finally see a path toward their calling and destiny. Though this topic throbs with deep anguish for people who are confused and aimless in life, it also vibrates with possibility and hope for those who are ready to step toward the calling they were made for.

So, yeah, this book is about the 6 Broken Places and the efforts that are necessary to heal them. But in the end . . . it's about you. It's about finding a broken place that resonates with what you were made to do in this life. When we take the broken places and begin to identify the traits and types of service that meet the needs to heal that brokenness, we find 6 main categories of people, and one or more might resonate with your soul's calling.

The 6 Broken Places	The 6 Callings
Injustice	Champions
Isolation	Nurturers
Pain	Healers
Decay	Stewards
Hatred	Activists
Separation	Ambassadors

Are you a CHAMPION? Do you see people struggling in situations that just shouldn't be, proclaim, "This is not right!," and set about trying to change the circumstance? If so, you might be a CHAMPION, fighting against INJUSTICE.

Are you a STEWARD? Does your heart break over the sight of our precious resources wasting away, and do you strive to be a conservationist to protect what God has given us? If so, you might be a STEWARD, preserving our world from DECAY.

Are you an ACTIVIST? Do you feel outrage over the division and animosity that keeps us from understanding and embracing differences, and do you stand up for those who don't have a voice? If so, you might be an ACTIVIST, seeking to combat HATRED.

Are you a HEALER? Do you see others suffering physically, mentally, or spiritually and look for ways to remedy the cause and eradicate the potential for it in the future? If so, you might be a HEALER, easing the world's PAIN.

Are you a NURTURER? Do you gravitate toward those who seem alone and lonely, who seem to have no one in their corner and who are afraid or don't know how to reach out? If so, you might be a NURTURER, bringing love and hope to those in ISOLATION.

Are you an AMBASSADOR? Do you feel led to reach out to those who may have lost their way and need to know the love of God? If so, you might be an AMBASSADOR, leading people out of SEPARATION.

Understanding the 6 Broken Places will help you identify what you were created to do in this life—where and how you were meant to serve and where you will hopefully see yourself and the traits you have that can bring relief to someone in one of those places.

These broken places are where you will . . .

. . . find your calling,

. . . discover your destiny,

. . . heal the world as one of God's deeply loved (and liked) masterpieces.

CHAPTER 2

THE CHAMPION

*"Because of the oppression of the weak and the groaning of
the needy, I will now arise," says the LORD. "I will protect them from those who malign them."*
—Psalm 12:5

There are no words for what I stared at as my jaw hit the
ground. I just could not grasp the enormity of the situation
which is Kibera. Like so many other visitors to Kenya before
me, I was taken to see Kibera, one of Nairobi's most expansive
neighborhoods and certainly one of the world's most enormous
slums. It is poverty on an unimaginable scale. We snaked
through the paths between hovels—the smells overwhelming,
the images searing. We were led to a small dark room and
ducked to enter. As my eyes adjusted to the dim light, I was
surprised to find about fifty kids crammed into this little
school. All in tattered clothes. No books. No paper. No pencils.
No blackboard. But this was their school. Leaving there, we
found our way to the corrugated-tin and mud-walled hut of a
woman on the last days of her fight against AIDS. She would
die soon and leave behind only a small pallet of a bed, a few
pots . . . and her middle-school-aged daughter. We offered
translated small talk and a desperate heartfelt prayer, and
then walked away.

Honestly the whole thing just did me in. I was wrecked.
My heart was crushed. I didn't say it out loud, but I certainly
thought it . . . this is just not right. None of it.

I so wish this was the only heart-crushing moment of its kind in my life, but, wow, it was far from it. I've had the privilege and burden of traveling around our country and internationally, seeing things through the eyes of our ministry partners. They didn't spare me any agony as I witnessed:

- A young boy begging on the streets of Islamabad, Pakistan, so severely disfigured that it turned my stomach. How do I describe this? His body was folded over backward, his feet reaching over his head, his stomach flat to the ground. And his hands were outstretched, asking for money. I was horrified. Again, I thought . . . *This is not right.*

- A line of kids from toddlers to teens queuing up for a few bites of rice and a teeny bit of mutton— their only meal of the day. Most of them were AIDS orphans, being raised by siblings in The Valley of 1000 Hills, South Africa. I had to wear my sunglasses to cover my tears. Again, *This is not right.*

- A room of Middle Eastern immigrant men sardined together with their meager belongings and a few mattresses into a tiny warehouse on the outskirts of Vienna—none of them documented—all waiting for a job or some kind of hope, anything to get them out of this purgatory, this waiting for months and months. I had one of the most remarkable conversations I've ever had about God with one of those men, but still, as I walked away, I thought . . . *This is not right.*

This is not right. NOT RIGHT! That's what I thought. That's what I felt. I was experiencing INJUSTICE.

I've seen injustice, I've heard injustice. I've even smelled it and tasted it. I'll bet you have too.

I hesitated about beginning with this broken place. I worried that it would be too overwhelming, and the scope and scale of it so impossible to get your minds around that it might simply be met with shoulder shrugs and cynicism. But I'm going to take a risk and start right here in this dark, broken place of INJUSTICE, not just because it is so prevalent in our world, but because many of you were designed by God before you were born to be CHAMPIONS of Justice. This is your calling . . . maybe your destiny. And the next few pages may be the finger in the chest you need to get in the game.

But let me try to make this broken place at least a little more accessible. I want to point out what I believe is at the heart of the injustice in our world. INJUSTICE is, in short, a state in which things . . . simply put . . . are just not right. When disadvantage is unequally distributed, when things are unfair and inequitable, when basic human rights are denied, or more generally, when some human beings' lives are not as they should be or could be, you find INJUSTICE. But I'm not talking about situations where your lifestyle isn't just what you want it to be, when you are marginally inconvenienced, or when someone says something mean to you. I am talking about a more pervasive problem that goes to the core of one's ability to have the basic necessities of life.

INJUSTICE takes many forms: abuse, exploitation, deprivation, persecution; but, at its heart, it is a form of bondage from which people find it hard to escape. And many times it is cyclical, passing on from one generation to the next. For many, injustice is inescapable without some kind of outside intervention. Maybe you have just what it takes to break that cycle for someone.

INJUSTICE is also systemic. It pervades cultures, families, countries. And it's insidious, hiding in human hearts and minds waiting to exploit lives. The Bible accurately refers to injustice in terms of yokes and chains. Where injustice dwells, people have no choice. They're stuck in it, most times for life.

Though there are many forms of injustice, there is one that often sets the stage for all the others: poverty. Poverty is, perhaps, the prime expression of INJUSTICE. Poverty is the lack of sufficient resources to keep body and soul together. Poverty makes all things worse and gives rise to dozens and dozens of other expressions of injustice. Here's one example. My son Barry, at the time a journalist with the organization he founded, World Next Door, told me of an uncomfortable dinner he experienced during his travels . He was shocked and sickened to learn that the Cambodian family with whom he was dining had been prostituting their own daughter for income to make ends meet. And there she was, sitting quietly across the table from him.

During the height of the AIDS crisis, I stood looking out over the wondrous beauty of the Kwa Zulu Natal region of South Africa and could not fathom that 2 out of 5 people living there would eventually be dead from AIDS—a disease that was fueled by unending cycles of poverty. I was devastated to learn I was standing near one of the mass graves where thousands of the poorest and nameless dead were stacked in unmarked trenches.

And, later, in 2011, one year after the 2010 earthquake in Haiti, I saw with my own eyes how insult upon insult was added to injury for these people. Already vulnerable under the weight of staggering poverty, corruption, and injustice, and despite millions of dollars of foreign aid and humanitarian efforts, Haiti was utterly devastated by the massive earthquake. Their dead were dump-trucked to a huge, unmarked mass grave. IDP (Internally Displaced People) camps sprung up everywhere. Buildings beyond repair leaned ominously. Contagious diseases multiplied and took further lives.

Each of these experiences compounded my already mounting sense that something had to be done as I continued to cry, "This isn't right!" The scale of injustice and injustice-induced tragedy all around us are more than we can fathom—more than we can stomach. If not outright sickened by the scope and scale of injustice, we, at the very least, are faced with a low-grade fever of sadness that persists day after day. And you don't have to see it with your own eyes, up close and personal. Just open your news app or preferred social media outlet, or go old school and watch the evening news. You'll quickly be reminded that injustice is happening . . . right now. Right now, a child is being trafficked. Right now, someone is becoming homeless. Right now, a baby is being aborted. Right now, a terrorist is donning a suicide vest. Right now, a human being is drinking disease-infested water. Right now, a toddler is dying of malnutrition. Right now, a woman is being beaten.

> "As long as poverty, injustice and gross inequity persist in our world, none of us can truly rest."
> —Nelson Mandela

Right now, a young girl is being denied education. Right now, a young boy is being turned into a child soldier.

Right now, everywhere, INJUSTICE . . . mind-blowing, heart-crushing injustice. So, what do we do about it? Can we do anything about it?

What Is a Champion?

Growing up, flannel-graph Jesus was the only version I knew—a millennial-looking, bearded white dude (he wasn't white, of course) who carried little lambkins on his shoulder and multiplied lunch when necessary. Oh, and, of course, he hung on a bloody cross to give me a shot at Heaven. That was my Jesus. That's the only Jesus I was taught. What I missed from Mrs. Truby's third grade Sunday School class, what she neglected to show me, was the Jesus who hung out with all the wrong people—the drunks, the women, the lepers, the kids, the half-breeds, the mentally ill, and the morally suspect. And, for sure, she never told me that Jesus expected us, His followers, to do the same. In all my years of Sunday School, and even into my years in Bible college and grad school, I was never, not once, introduced to the Jesus who was incredibly political and so concerned about social justice. If I saw the words of Isaiah and Jesus, instructing us in this regard, I certainly didn't understand them in terms of injustice. All my Bible gurus told me that Jesus was spiritualizing Isaiah's words. He meant spiritually blind, spiritually poor, spiritually captive—he didn't mean those literally suffering.

But they were dead wrong, as evidenced in Jesus' further thoughts on the subject. Look at what he told a rich young man:

> Someone came to Jesus with this question: "Teacher, what good deed must I do to have eternal life?" "Why ask me about what is good?" Jesus replied. "There is only One who is good. But to answer your question—if you want to receive eternal life, keep the commandments." "Which ones?" the man asked. And Jesus replied: "'You must not murder. You must not commit

adultery. You must not steal. You must not testify falsely. Honor your father and mother. Love your neighbor as yourself.'" "I've obeyed all these commandments," the young man replied. "What else must I do?" Jesus told him, "If you want to be perfect, go and sell all your possessions and give the money to the poor, and you will have treasure in Heaven. Then come, follow me." But when the young man heard this, he went away very sad, for he had many possessions.

—Matthew 19:16-22

Sell it all, give it to the poor, and come follow me. You may be tempted to spiritualize this too, but the uncomfortable truth is that he wasn't exaggerating. He meant it because he cared so much about justice.

Perhaps the most poignant insights from Jesus about the topic of those struggling under the weight of injustice were these:

For I was hungry, and you fed me. I was thirsty, and you gave me a drink. I was a stranger, and you invited me into your home. I was naked, and you gave me clothing. I was sick, and you cared for me. I was in prison, and you visited me.

—Matthew 25:35-36

And the King will say, "I tell you the truth, when you did it to one of the least of these my brothers and sisters, you were doing it to me!"

—Matthew 25:40

Jesus, looking to a future moment when God would execute judgment upon human beings for how they treated the disenfranchised and needy, actually radically identified with them. He said, "Any act of loving justice you offer to the marginalized you offer to me! That's me there . . . the naked guy! That's me over there . . . the poor woman. That's me there . . . that teenager in prison."

It is unequivocal. Jesus didn't just care about INJUSTICE; its eradication was a huge part of his calling and at the heart of the mission he passed on to his followers. And in the years following his death, resurrection, and ascension, his followers, who became the church's early leaders, made sure to include justice as one of the church's main responsibilities.

- Suppose there are brothers or sisters who need clothes and don't have enough to eat. What good is there in your saying to them, "God bless you! Keep warm and eat well!" if you don't give them the necessities of life? (James 2:15-16)

- There were no needy people among them, because those who owned land or houses would sell them and bring the money to the apostles to give to those in need. (Acts 4:34-35)

- Pure and genuine religion in the sight of God the Father means caring for orphans and widows in their distress and refusing to let the world corrupt you. (James 1:27)

- If someone has enough money to live well and sees a brother or sister in need but shows no compassion—how can God's love be in that person? Dear children, let's not merely say that we love each other; let us show the truth by our actions. Our actions will show that we belong to the truth, so we will be confident when we stand before God. (1 John 3:17-19)

Your actions—your efforts to bring healing to the broken place of INJUSTICE—will show that you belong to the truth. Your commitment to justice will give evidence to the faith you so boldly proclaim. Then, someday, when you face God himself, he will have noticed!

And, when Jesus made his big statement of purpose and mission, he simply quoted Isaiah:

The Spirit of the LORD is upon me, for he has anointed me to bring Good News to the poor. He has sent me to proclaim that captives will be released, that the blind will see, that the oppressed will be set free, and that the time of the LORD's favor has come. (Luke 4:18-19)

Champions are the people who see INJUSTICE and won't tolerate it. They answer the call to see that wrongs are righted, that suffering is ended, that the mission Jesus had here is continued. Now, let me tell you about some folks who have taken that call seriously.

Champions: Healers of Injustice

You might think becoming a champion of justice is a calling only for people with endless resources, powerful connections, or special skills, but you'd be wrong. First, it is important to understand that if you are made with a calling, you are also equipped with what you need to fulfill it, even if you don't see it in yourself yet or fear the magnitude of what you feel compelled to do. Second, the only thing you really need in order to step up and be a champion is to acknowledge your desire to make a difference—to make things right—and to be willing to act on that desire.

However, you should understand that there are obstacles to stepping into a calling when you are dealing with broken people in a broken place. We will see as we visit each of these places how there are societal stigmas—perceived or real—that keep those suffering from asking for help and, therefore, stand in the way of those who would help from fully understanding what they need or how to remedy it. INJUSTICE may not seem like one of those cases where people are afraid to talk about what they are enduring, but how often do we see someone in crisis and discover they have been in that situation for a long time without our knowledge? Many times, people feel their problems are either too insignificant to bother someone else with them or too huge for anyone to be able to help, so they suffer in silence. Whether it is because they don't feel deserving or fear being rejected when they ask for help, there are many things that just are not right that are tolerated because the stigma of being vulnerable and in need permeates nearly every culture. The poor and downtrodden are pitied. Who wants to be pitied?

If you feel led to respond to the calling of being a CHAMPION for Justice, you may face your own feelings of being overwhelmed by the sheer magnitude of the need. You may also encounter resistance in the form of pride, mistrust, or hopelessness, but that is not a reason to back away. In fact, it is all the more reason to lean in.

The stories that follow are of average people who have done extraordinary things because they recognized that calling in their lives and chose to respond. I hope you will find inspiration here and maybe see yourself in one of them and take their lead.

CHUCK AND VIVIAN GROSS

Most folks at Chuck and Vivian's stage of life are slowing down. Not them. Nope. They seem to be speeding up! As other retirees shift their focus to hobbies and pastimes, Chuck and Vivian have become justice champions! They are shining examples of what it means to live into your destiny. They are living proof that personal impact has no shelf-life. And they give me hope that the church, with enough Chuck and Vivians leading the way, can have a huge impact in healing injustice.

For Chuck and Vivian, there has been no confusion in their minds as to the needs of the hour. They absolutely do not equivocate about what to do with their lives. Commitment to the cause of Jesus—particularly in bringing healing to the broken place of INJUSTICE—is what they live for. They are my heroes!

But they didn't used to be this way. Chuck will tell you that, prior to relocating from southern California to central Indiana, he had a negative attitude about the poor. He thought, *It is your fault you are where you are.* And he'll admit he was confused. "I couldn't get perspective on the scale of the needs in injustice." He says the best he could do was throw money at the problem. He now sees how he and Vivian were living with an old paradigm of calling, and explains, "Now I'm an Ephesians 2:10 guy. I have no excuse anymore."

Vivian had other struggles when it came to engaging in meeting others' needs. She, like half of America, is an introvert. An introvert who admits, "I don't have much self-confidence." Until they moved to Indiana this kept her on the sidelines of justice as well. She just didn't see where she could be involved, and no one asked her! But, a time finally came when Vivian saw an opportunity, was asked to step out in faith, and, though she'd never say this about herself, is now a justice CHAMPION in our church community!

Chuck and Vivian have realized they still have callings to fulfill. They have destinies to discover, not a retirement to relax into. Chuck says, "Grace Church made it crystal clear we were to help others." And now that they are, he says, "It's addictive!"

Here are just some of the ways Chuck and Vivian have sought to bring healing to the broken place of INJUSTICE. They've become Guardians Ad Litem, court-appointed representatives who look out for the legal interests of infants and children who need someone to protect their rights. Vivian was captivated and deeply concerned by something she read about in the paper—children and infants who, for various reasons, were stuck in the legal system and had no voice for themselves. Vivian realized there was a great need for such guardians in divorce, neglect, and abuse cases. Right away, she felt as if God was in it. She says, "God put us together (with a particular child) and God used me. I realized introverts can be used!"

From this beginning in justice ministry, Chuck and Vivian went deeper into caring for at-risk children and families. They became a Safe Family. Safe Families for Children is an organization that works with the church to raise up folks who will take in at-risk children for set periods while their families are in a time of struggle. It helps that family and those children avoid the foster system. Chuck and Vivian became one such Safe Family. I'll never forget the image of Vivian standing in our church lobby lovingly holding one of those tiny children in her arms.

Then there's their tireless work in our Care Center. The Grace Care Center exists to help people in our community through a choice food pantry, referral and vehicle services, and ESL (English as a Second Language) classes. Chuck and Vivian serve our friends of the Care Center weekly in a variety of capacities. Chuck seems to be everywhere at the Care Center, loving on people, guiding them, and pastoring them. He's like a personal ambassador for each friend of the Care Center that he meets. Truly remarkable.

How they find time for anything else is beyond me, but they do. They help lead a gathering of seniors from our community called Together Today—a program of the Shepherd Center of Hamilton County. Here Chuck and Vivian throw themselves into yet another broken place: ISOLATION, which is a perpetual problem of the elderly in America. (More on that broken place later.) They also have found great joy in going on mission trips to Central America with Bridges of Hope International. Vivian has gone five times!

See what I mean about them? Unambiguously committed to healing the broken place of INJUSTICE. They are living out of calling and stepping into their destiny. And so could you!

KIRSTEN AND MARCUS CASTEEL

And then there's this story of how two CHAMPIONS met, fell in love, and launched a new family into healing the broken places of this world! Let's begin with Kirsten. Kirsten would tell you that in the fall of 2007 her "life was a complete mess." Having just ended a relationship and looking to create a home for her son that better reflected Christian values, she showed up at our church. Shortly thereafter, responding to an offer to participate in a mission trip to New York City with New York City Relief, she came face to face with both the state of her heart and the state of the world. Here's how she explains what happened to her on the streets of New York:

> We were in the heart of Harlem, outside of an hourly motel. For that few hours we were there, I remember seeing a woman walk in and out of that hourly motel with different men. I would cry every time I saw her, and I just remember being very aware that I couldn't believe what I was experiencing. This is something you would see on TV! I felt two overwhelming feelings. I thought, *My gosh, I could be in that situation. That's not somebody else; that's any one of us.* Then I realized I could not fix her situation. It was in that moment I felt God calling me . . . calling me to, at the very least, love her and the others around us on the street. That trip was, for me, really the start of everything changing because I came home and threw myself into the work of justice in my own city, Indianapolis.

Kirsten became a CHAMPION on the streets of Harlem. Little did she know that her future husband was going through his own transformation. Marcus had served for six years as a leader on our church's annual high school mission trip to Canton, Mississippi. There he saw poverty and racism in all its ugliness and tragedy. He said it "literally was as if you went back in time" to the Jim Crow years in the South. He'll tell you he saw "extreme poverty and direct segregation" going on before his eyes. He observed numerous kids without shoes, houses with a dozen buckets inside to catch the rain, a home burning to the ground because the fire department wouldn't service outside the city limits, and stop signs so shot up that you couldn't read the word "STOP." And, in a moment of foreshadowing, he was struck with the fact that so many of the kids he was ministering to were fatherless. He'll tell you, "All this did something to me." In Marcus, another CHAMPION for justice was born.

Both Marcus and Kirsten wrestled with the question: "How can you help in your own backyard?" They both threw themselves into answering it. Over the next ten years, their lives went into overdrive for justice. Kirsten continued the street ministry in New York and became the trips' most ardent leader. But not satisfied with this, she found a way to reshape her job at Eli Lilly, in time, becoming the firm's Global Philanthropy Consultant. She now mobilizes tens of thousands of Lilly employees to contribute and engage in the work of justice all over the world.

Meanwhile, Marcus, still haunted by the notion that so many kids have no dads, determined, as a single man, to sign up to be a Safe Family. We all were amazed to watch Marcus take in and then adopt the twin teen boys Devonta and Javonta. I am still in awe of his courage. He truly lived "brave not safe"! Then, Marcus took on the task of mobilizing our church to feed the hungry in our county (the wealthiest in Indiana). In a very long story made short, over the last six years, Marcus has led the creation of the Grace Care Center, which meets the physical, emotional, financial, and ultimately, spiritual needs of thousands of our friends living around us. He has created the most sustainable successful care-giving model I have ever seen in my life.

Marcus and Kirsten were mobilizing thousands upon thousands of people to get in the game of justice. They were creating CHAMPIONS! And then they met each other. And they fell in love. And they married. And now they are creating a family of Justice CHAMPIONS. In recent days, they've become foster parents solely to adopt. And by the time you read this book, little Devon will have become a Casteel. I tear up even as I write this. Marcus, Kirsten, Devonta, Javonta, Brennan, and Devon Casteel. A family of CHAMPIONS for Justice. And my heroes.

Marcus is matter of fact about it all. He told me, "Nothing's too small that will change the world."

EMILY DELDAR

"I want to establish a lifestyle of good oral health care all over the world!" Those are not the kinds of words you would expect to hear coming out of the mouth of a typical sixteen-year-old American girl. But, then again, Emily Deldar is anything but typical. Emily wants to change the world and do it in a very specific way . . . through toothbrushes!

Emily is a good student. She's bright, intelligent, and gifted. But she is also passionate and driven. Growing up as the child of a mom and dad who are both dentists, she of course knew all about good oral health. Under their influence she had been thinking of a career in medicine, perhaps orthodontia, following in their footsteps.

But in a short six-month span her focus turned from career to calling. She's pretty young to be thinking such grand and passionate thoughts, don't you think? But it makes sense when you see the journey she has been on.

In the summer of 2018 Emily was invited to be her high school's representative at the Congress of Future Medical Leaders in Boston. There she was inspired by powerful speakers who shared their own stories of doing big things for humanity while they were still quite young. Emily felt moved to do the same but had no idea what that might be. The final speaker of the conference, Sean Stephenson, ignited her passion further when he told the attendees, "You can do whatever you want no matter what is in your way! What you were meant to do will overcome the obstacles!"

The final turning point in her journey came later that summer as she listened to me give a sermon on the topic of "You were Made for More!" That afternoon she went home thinking, *I'm in . . . but what can I do with myself?* She began mulling over her potential, her passions, and her interests and started doing research. She discovered a truth that set her back. One half of the people in the world do not own a toothbrush! She discovered that the lack of sufficient oral care and multiple people sharing toothbrushes led to the advancement of numerous diseases.

In rapid order she determined God would have her launch her own non-profit organization that could begin to solve some of the oral health problems of the developing world. A child of her generation, she did what she knew to do . . . she Googled "How to start a non-profit organization." Emily searched for non-profits in the Indianapolis area, began writing to as many of them as she could to ask for their help, and simply assumed somebody would step up to give her guidance. Somebody did. Dick and Suzi Stephens, CO-Founders of The Malawi Project came alongside of Emily and guided her on the formation of The World Smiles Mission.

Emily dutifully did all the paper work, (got IRS approval in an unheard of nine days), formed a board (the girls she ate lunch with), opened a bank account (with her dad as the treasurer), and started collecting toothbrushes and toothpaste to send all over the world (by calling every dentist's office in Central Indiana to ask for donations!).

Even before she had finalized the details of her new 501c3 organization, Emily sent her first shipment of toothbrushes and toothpaste to Malawi! In months she had moved from dream to reality!

What sixteen-year-old does this? Emily does.

How to Step into Your Champion Calling

Are you inspired? I hope so! As you work your way through this book from one broken place to the next, you will discover more people just like Chuck, Vivian, Kirsten, and Marcus. I hope they stimulate your imagination and motivate you to action! Whether it's in INJUSTICE or PAIN or HATRED or DECAY or ISOLATION or SEPARATION, you'll dive further into your calling because of their examples.

As you reflect on the numerous stories of real people in the book I want you to note two attributes common to them all. First, note their courage. At some point along the way they adopted this posture: *Live brave, not safe!* This is the short, snappy, and powerful battle cry I first heard from Gary Haugen, CEO and Founder of the International Justice Museum. I will likely never forget it and I hope neither will you.

> Here is one choice that our Father wants us to understand as Christians – and I believe this is the choice of our age: Do we want to be brave or safe? Gently, lovingly, our heavenly Father wants us to know that we simply can't be both.

> —Gary Haugen[8]

No matter what you choose to do to get the job done, to get in the game and to fulfill your calling . . . DO NOT PLAY IT SAFE! Do the brave thing. Give the outlandish amount of money. Go to the most ridiculous lengths. Live bravely. Display your heart right out there on your sleeve.

There is another trait common to everyone who would seek to live out their God-given destiny. You can see it in all the stories within this book. It is a commitment to take one step at a time. My son Barry, in his memoir, *Into the World Next Door: Stories of Hope and Adventure from an Unlikely Journey Around the World*, describes this one-step-at-a-time obedience as "the Path of Yes."

> **"How does one even begin to live in a world-changing life of faith? . . . They don't ask questions. They simply take the next step . . . walking the 'Path of Yes.'"**

"How does one even begin to live a world-changing life of faith? How do you become a normal follower of Christ? The answer, I now believe, lies in a word I've heard spoken many times by the amazing Christ-followers I've encountered around the world. It's a word they seem to be in the habit of saying loudly and often. The word is "YES." It seems that every time God calls them to take a step of faith, their consistent, trusting answer is always the same: "Yes, Lord. I'll go." They don't ask questions. They don't raise concerns. They simply take the next step in their faith journey and God meets them along the way. I call the road they're walking the "Path of Yes."

—Barry Rodriguez[9]

There it is. A balance. On one hand, to live out your destiny will require a courage that, at times, borders on the heroic. On the other hand, it's just waking up tomorrow and doing the next right thing.

So, do you want to get started healing INJUSTICE? Feeling the urge to take the path of "yes"? Then here are some ways you can get moving.

PARTNER WITH OTHER CHAMPIONS

Honestly, the quickest, and perhaps the simplest way for you to begin bringing healing to INJUSTICE is to find an organization whose mission and values resonate with your heart. You can get behind them because you dig their vision and you respect their leadership. And they get the job done!

Partnering, of course, includes contributing financially to their cause. The vast majority of these kinds of organizations are nonprofit. They live and die on the generosity of others like you, so don't be stingy. How much should you be giving? Well, that's a decision you'll have to make on your own; but, a good rule of thumb is to give 10% of your gross income to an organization with whom you have chosen to partner.

Beyond giving, partnering with like-minded, like-hearted organizations should involve your time and physical labor. These hard-working organizations always need people to help in a myriad of ways. If you resonate with them, call them, text them, write them, and ask, "Hey, what can I do to help?" Now, listen to me here: their initial reaction will be mixed. They will, of course, be thrilled to know others share their burden, but be patient; some of these movements struggle with placing and supporting volunteers since they spend most of their time just doing their thing. And if they aren't ready to get you in the game, that's cool; there are plenty of others out there waiting with open arms.

One of the best ways to partner with an organization dedicated to healing one of the 6 Broken Places is to do a short-term mission trip with them. You should know, though, it is sometimes strenuous and heart-wrenching; but wow, it can be a full-immersion, broken-place healing exercise.

Just a couple of illustrations from my own experience: The sights, sounds, and feelings of walking through a Haitian village in a serving opportunity I had with Nehemiah Vision Ministry are implanted in my memory. I'll also always cherish the conversations in Manhattan with some amazing homeless folks during my mission trip with New York City Relief. I often recall having tea in a remote Pakistani village with a gracious family to whom we were introduced. These and many others helped shape my world view and my calling. But I think I need to take a bit of a rabbit trail and address something crucial you need to understand about taking mission trips and serving, in general. It's this: When you serve, serve humbly. When you go, go open-palmed as a learner, not as a fixer.

The poor are not a problem to solve. They are fellow image-bearers of God who, like you, need to be loved and, ultimately, transformed. So, as you serve, yes, do so with passion and energy, but also with humility. Show up. Care. Listen. Love. And look for Jesus. You're going to see him!

One last thought on finding a partner organization. There are literally tens of thousands of justice-related ministries and organizations in need of support. There are huge, world-wide organizations doing incredible work like International Justice Mission, Compassion International, World Vision, and KIVA, just to name a few. Then there are the many local CHAMPIONS of Justice right around the corner from where you live. A simple Google search might be all you need. Do your homework. What are the justice needs in your community? Then rally the troops, your friends, your relatives, your church family, and your pastor! Start something and watch it grow!

Our church has dozens of justice ministry partners, a number of which began from our own people getting worked up about poverty or hunger or adoption or food rescue. And these partners do an incredible job involving our people in all sorts of Kingdom work. But, by far, the biggest justice ministry supported by our people is our own Grace Care Center. Hundreds of our church family serve weekly in the Care Center's Choice Food Pantry, Car Care Ministry, Referral Ministry, and ESL classes. It began very small, but today the center touches the lives of over 500 families per week in central Indiana. It is the most sustainable people-care justice ministry I have personally encountered. And, it can be replicated. You can do the very same thing in your own church . . . and we'll gladly show you how!

PRAY FOR THE HEALING OF INJUSTICE
In his incredible book *The Meaning of Prayer*, written in 1915, Harry Fosdick suggests there are three ways God gets stuff done in the world: when human beings think, when human beings work, and when human beings pray.

> The mystery of prayer's projectile force is great, but the certainty of such prayer's influence, one way or another, in working redemption for needy lives is greater still[10].

The scope and scale of injustice almost makes praying for it an impossibly huge task. But we must, because "Prayer is not only universal in extent; it is infinite in quality."[11]

Prayer is one way for us to develop what Gary Haugen calls "compassion permanence."

> Perhaps a next step in our development as children of God is a capacity for compassion permanence—a courageous and generous capacity to remember the needs of an unjust world even when they are out of our immediate sight. It is not our first and most natural inclination to reserve a space in our thought life for those who suffer abuse and oppression in our world.[12]

Here are just a small handful of ways you could incorporate prayer for injustice into your life:

- Begin a justice prayer journal, notebook, or scrapbook.

- Subscribe to your partner organization's emails—they'll be loaded with ways to pray.

- Form a prayer team around an issue of injustice that moves you.

There really is only one foolproof way to get better at praying for justice and righteousness in the world . . . just do it. And when you begin to pray, wielding what Fosdick calls the "projectile power of intercession," you will be standing in the gap on behalf of God.

I looked for someone who might rebuild the wall
of righteousness that guards the land. I searched
for someone to stand in the gap in the wall . . .
but I found no one.

—Ezekiel 22:30

LEARN AND GROW IN YOUR CALLING

Vision leaks. Have you heard that before? It means that life
has a way of requiring so much of our time, energy, interest,
and resources that even a heart full of passion for justice can
begin to lose its fullness.

The passion leaks out of the spaces that are created by
the strain and pull of the demands life makes on us.

The quickest, most surefire way to refuel your
commitment to healing INJUSTICE is to get engaged, get in
the game . . . do something! But, short of that, here are a few
other ways you can refill your heart with the drive to meet
injustice head on.

Read and learn. Here are some books I've read that
have had a lasting impact on my thinking and praying about
INJUSTICE:

- Pretty much anything by Gary Haugen, CEO of
  International Justice Mission. Especially helpful was *Good News About Injustice.*

- *Rich Christians in an Age of Hunger* by Ronald
  Sider

- *The End of Poverty* by Jeffrey Sachs

- *Shaking the System* by Tim Stafford

- *Nickel and Dimed* by Barbara Ehrenreich

- *The Hole in our Gospel* by Richard Stearns

And do not miss this one: *When Helping Hurts* by Steve Corbett and Brian Fikkert. It is a must-read for anyone with half a passion for tackling injustice. It will provide a needed corrective for errant views of poverty that perpetuate unhealthy cycles of hurting the poor and ourselves while trying to alleviate the problem.

Watch and learn . . . and cringe and weep. I've found a handful of films, some independently created and some big-budget Hollywood productions, that are deeply stimulating and deeply disturbing. All of these films have had a profound impact on me and my thinking about injustice.

Caution: These are, largely, not appropriate for kids, nor for the squeamish and faint of heart! Some of these films are (appropriately) R-rated and include sexuality, intense language, disturbing images and concepts, along with graphic violence. Please be forewarned!

- *Tears of the Sun*
- *Beyond Borders*
- *The Constant Gardener*
- *Yesterday*
- *Rabbit Proof Fence*
- *Blood Diamond*
- *In America*
- *Beasts of No Nation*

One more time for good measure . . . please be aware of the intensity of these films! Skip the popcorn, but prepare for heart change!

MAKE SIGNIFICANT LIFESTYLE ADJUSTMENTS
This is where things get a little less easy and a little less comfortable, but I have confidence in your ability to handle it. If you want to make serious attempts at healing INJUSTICE, you are going to want to free up some of your financial resources to be able to invest them where needed. And you know what that means; you need to simplify your life and downsize your material appetite. I can only touch on a few broad-stroke ideas, but maybe this will get you thinking and planning:

- Buy less, buy smaller, buy less frequently.

- Scale back on big purchases—houses, cars, education, weddings, vacations.

- Substitute generosity for spending. I've been moved by the number of young kids who have asked for no gifts at their birthday parties and instead asked for food for a food pantry; I also know of a number of families who gave up vacations to raise funds for a partner ministry and still others who completely replaced Christmas gift exchanges with generous acts of giving.

If you are going to be about justice, you are going to have to budget for it!

There is another benefit to making significant financial lifestyle adjustments. It will not only free up finances to better support justice organizations, but it will also help you and your family better live in mindful empathy with those who suffer from injustice.

DO RANDOM BUT THOUGHTFUL ACTS

This is where it gets fun. Keep your eyes open for signs of injustice and be prepared to act. For instance, here's a story I watched play out before me on the streets of Chicago.

Walking down the sidewalk, I noticed a young man bend down and give a homeless man a gift card to a restaurant nearby. (I could see the logo on the card). Piecing it together in my mind, what I believe I was observing was that the young man noticed the homeless guy as he walked to lunch. As he ordered his own meal, he bought a gift card at the same time; and then, on his way back to work offered the gift to the man. Random act of justice, yes. But thoughtful and pre-meditated, too!

Pay attention. Look. Listen. And when you see something that is within your power to change, take action. Just do it.

ESTABLISH RELATIONSHIPS

If you are going to become a CHAMPION against INJUSTICE, you need to know what it feels like to live with it. What better way to learn than to walk alongside those who struggle mightily with it daily? Look around you and seek out people and organizations that regularly face INJUSTICE. But don't go into this to solve their dilemma; just love and listen.

A simple start is to purposely spend time outside of your normal geographical community. I've done a lot of the writing of this book at the main public library in downtown Indy. It has allowed me to rub shoulders with folks I'd rarely connect with in my usual haunts. Visit a senior living community or an inmate in a correctional facility. Volunteer in an urban school district or at a local soup kitchen. The point is to get out of your comfort zone because that is where you will encounter the discomfort others live with.

BECOME A PUBLIC ADVOCATE

Harness the power of social media and speak to your sphere of influence. Write a blog. Engage in social activism. Host a viewing party of one of the films listed previously. Start a justice book club.

It's great to be passionate about stopping injustice, but if you don't use the voice you have and the privilege and influence that is yours , then you aren't truly a CHAMPION. Stepping into your calling means embracing your ability to say and do something when you notice injustice. Speak up, draw other people's attention to the need and ask for their support of your efforts.

BRING OTHERS ON BOARD

You can involve friends and family, but an even better way to maximize your efforts is to get your company involved and establish a corporate policy of social responsibility. If you inspire your people to see the link between healing the world and maintaining the bottom line of your business, you'll have employees who go home every day not only feeling that they advanced the company's mission, but also changed the world while finding their destiny in the mix! A win, win, for sure.

Is there an area of justice that your company can resonate with? Is there some act of justice you and your people can do together that is commensurate with your business vision?

Go back and read the story of how Jeff Simmons is doing this with Elanco. Here, too, are a few examples of other companies that have melded their corporate bottom line with a holistic view of healing INJUSTICE in the world:

Elanco – Elanco has set a company goal to break the cycle of hunger in 100 communities around the world. They fly employees, as well as customers, to those cities to roll up their sleeves and make hunger a non-issue for one year for many families. From Anderson, IN to Seattle, WA to cities in China and others in Cambodia, Elanco's employees are seeing the broken place of INJUSTICE up close, but also learning the resolution.

Toms – The "One for One" motto is a well-known phrase; Toms recently upped the ante by donating a portion of their sunglasses sales to vision care for children in need. But it's not just consumers that are involved in Toms' social good, it's their employees as well. Toms' employees participate in an annual Shoe Drop where they travel and donate a variety of goods to children.

LinkedIn - One Friday each month, LinkedIn's employees participate in "InDay." InDay's purpose is to give back to the community through employee volunteerism and resources. Each InDay has a different theme, allowing diverse departments to come together for a common cause.

PG&E – This utility company does more than service the communities of California. On Earth Day, employees help clean and restore eighteen state parks. They are exemplary members of Habitat for Humanity and volunteer by providing solar panels on new Habitat homes. Employee volunteerism hits inside the home as well, as they participate in various food programs, providing those struggling to make ends meet with care packages and thousands of pounds of groceries.

Zappos – This company is creating a social impact with a shoebox. Zappos is known for a company culture that focuses on the well being of their employees, and they are on a mission to make the world a better place for everyone. They also donate huge amounts of Zappos' goods to lots of charitable organizations. Their employees are paid for time off if they are volunteering because Zappos knows 9-5 isn't the only work that matters.

General Electric – The employees of this multinational company volunteer over 1 million hours per year! Donations from the GE foundation have supported senior centers, children with autism, literacy programs, and neglected urban spaces among many other programs.

You, Again

I'm going to close this chapter with a reminder of two things. First, you are a masterpiece of God. You were created before your body, personality, and brain were even added. And even in that bodiless state, God saw amazing potential in you. Maybe it was to bring healing to the INJUSTICE of the world. Are you wired to be a CHAMPION? Look inside . . . no, feel inside. Does bone-crushing poverty disturb you? Do you get worked up easily over the marginalization of others? Do you weep when you see desperate images out of war-ravaged Syria or South Sudan or the streets of New York?

Maybe you were made for this.

Second, if you were, you can't say no. You were created to do the good works of God embodied in his Kingdom's expansion. If God gifted you to fight INJUSTICE, then he expects you'll do just that. But, don't let that overwhelm or intimidate you. Remember, as I said earlier, if God made you for it, he equipped you for it too. You just have to open yourself up to discovering what your skills and gifts are and how they align with this passion.

Maybe this is where your destiny and the world's great needs meet. What do you think?

CHAPTER 3
NURTURERS

"Loneliness is the first thing that God named 'not good.'"
—Thomas Merton

According to the people of both *Money* and *Town and Country* magazines, the city where I live is one of the best areas of the country. Over the last few years, the northern suburbs of Indianapolis have received numerous accolades, touting it as "an irresistible draw for families" and "an ideal place to work and play." And, yeah, it is kind of nice around here with good schools, arts, sports, shopping, lower crime, etc. But these honors belie a less acknowledged reality: even with all of this "pleasantness," this is an incredibly lonely place. We are no different from every other community in America,, whether in the top ten or bottom ten of somebody's ranking.

Loneliness is common because isolation is a normal state these days. And it is hurting us . . . deeply. ISOLATION is clearly a broken place in the tony suburbs of America. Here are a few cases in point: Recently a man walked off the street into our church and told one of our pastors who sat down with him, "I've been trying to get myself to stop at Grace Church for months. Today was a particularly difficult day, so I left work early to come by since I was so desperate to talk to someone. I have been a functional alcoholic since I was fourteen years old. I was raised Catholic but have only been to Mass a couple of times in thirty years. I tried to go to Mass recently, but couldn't make it through the service. My life is falling apart. I don't belong anywhere, and I need a community. My family needs a community." Kevin, our campus pastor, told me later, "I have rarely talked with someone who had this mixture of raw brokenness, honesty, and clarity about what he really needed."

One of the most heartbreaking examples I've seen (that thankfully has a happy ending) is a man who, for all of his life, has lived physically limited to his wheelchair. For years, he made it through life on his own while suffering with debilitating sadness and fighting for the will to live. Bitter toward God, he let himself go spiraling into depression and a "who cares" attitude about life. Fortunately, at the time he reached his lowest point, our church was launching a new initiative designed to direct people into community and relationships. He took a chance and joined. He now has a spiritual family. One I believe saved his life. But he is the exception.

Isolation and the lack of loving relationships or significant community affects all ages and all stages of life. Particularly hard hit, though, are kids and the elderly. One of the most disturbing moments in my life was the day my mom returned from a visit with my grandparents in Florida. Her parents had moved south years before, and more or less lived isolated and alone thereafter. My mom looked shellshocked as she described what she discovered: my grandma in a horrific physical and mental state, neglected and abused, clinging to life. I so wish this was an aberration, but from all I hear, it is simply not unusual for seniors to suffer from severe isolation. I won't forget my neighbor Bob talking about his own 100+ yr old mother and how the older she got the more the circle around her—her world—shrunk until very little was left but her and a few relatives. I believe she lived as long as she did because Bob, himself a senior, faithfully loved and cared for her and refused for her to live completely isolated.

According to the U.S. Census Bureau 11 million (28 percent) of people aged sixty-five and older lived alone at the time of the last census. As people get older, their likelihood of living alone only increases. Additionally, more and more older adults do not have children, reports the AARP, and that means fewer family members to provide company and care as those adults become seniors. Many studies show a connection between social isolation and higher rates of elder abuse. Whether this is because isolated adults are more likely to fall victim to abuse, or is a result of abusers attempting to isolate the elders from others to minimize risk of discovery, researchers aren't certain.

In children, it leads to all kinds of problems. Failure to be socially connected to peers is the real reason behind most school dropouts. It sets in motion a course on which children spin their way to outcast status and develop delinquency and other forms of antisocial behavior. One form of childhood isolation, in particular, has had a profound effect on kids: the dissolution of marriages. Fifteen million U.S. children, or 1 in 3, live without a father, and nearly 5 million live without a mother. In 1960, just 11 percent of American children lived in homes without fathers. Many problems in our culture can be directly or indirectly traced to fatherlessness in one form or another. Michael (I've changed his name) comes to mind. Abandoned early in life, Michael was thrown into the foster system, bouncing from house to house, threatened, beaten, stunted in all ways. Even when taken into a loving home of friends of mine and given every kind of love and care a kid could need, Michael was so wounded that he could not stop himself from lashing out at everyone around him. Freaked out and haunted by terrible memories, he became a danger to all. He had to be sent into high-risk foster care. I'm not sure what will become of him.

The statistics of the impact of this kind of isolation on kids are staggering:

- Living in a single-parent home doubles the risk that a child will suffer physical, emotional, or educational neglect.

- 63% of youth suicide victims are from fatherless homes—5 times the average.

- 90% of all homeless and runaway children are from fatherless homes—32 times the average.

- 85% of all children who show behavior disorders come from fatherless homes—20 times the average

- 75% of all adolescent patients in chemical abuse centers come from fatherless homes—10 times the average.

- Children who live without their biological fathers are, on average, at least two to three times more likely to be poor, to use drugs, to experience educational, health, emotional, and behavioral problems, to be victims of child abuse, and to engage in criminal behavior than their peers who live with their married, biological (or adoptive) parents.[13]

Jay Height is a friend of mine who leads an urban ministry on the near-east side of Indianapolis and is in constant contact with the police department. He recently told me that eight out of ten calls to the Indianapolis Police Department are somehow related to loneliness. Jay said, "People don't know who to turn to when they have a need." And let's be honest about something here. This ISOLATION problem (like *all* of the broken places) is of our own making. Americans cling like mad to the myth of the outsider . . . the desire to be the hero who stands apart from the crowd. And we hang on to an intense cultural individualism that may be more American than apple pie. We highly value working alone from home. And we buy into what author Barbara Ehrenreich calls "the cult of busyness." We are deliberately frenetic and over-scheduled. All of this pushes us to the fringes of community, out where we are not known nor want to be known.

So, just how commonplace is loneliness and isolation? A poll conducted for the Cigna Corporation, a global health service company, in May of 2018 indicates that nearly half the nation struggled with it. The evaluation of loneliness was measured on the UCLA Loneliness Scale, a frequently referenced and acknowledged academic measure used to gauge loneliness.

The survey of more than 20,000 U.S. adults ages eighteen years and older revealed some alarming findings:

- Nearly half of Americans report sometimes or always feeling alone (46 percent) or left out (47 percent).

- One in four Americans (27 percent) rarely or never feel as though there are people who really understand them.

- Two in five Americans sometimes or always feel that their relationships are not meaningful (43 percent) and that they are isolated from others (43 percent).

- One in five people report they rarely or never feel close to people (20 percent) or feel like there are people they can talk to (18 percent).

- Only half of Americans (53 percent) have meaningful in-person social interactions, such as having an extended conversation with a friend or spending quality time with family on a daily basis.

- Generation Z (adults ages 18-22) is the loneliest generation and claims to be in worse health than older generations.

- Social media use alone is not a predictor of loneliness; respondents defined as very heavy users of social media have a loneliness score (43.5) that is not markedly different from the score of those who never use social media (41.7).[14]

The crazy thing about our growing isolation is that we feel more "connected" than ever. In some ways you could say that more of us than ever are "known." I used quotation marks because we really aren't known, and certainly not connected, despite our social media saturation. A recent Pew research study noted that on a total population basis (accounting for Americans who do not use the internet at all), 68 percent of all U.S. adults are Facebook users, 28 percent use Instagram, 26 percent use Pinterest, 25 percent use LinkedIn and 21 percent use Twitter. That may be "us" on those pages and in those tweets and in those pics, but they are more like caricatures or dimensions or facsimiles or ruses. He was referring to his personal fame, I know, but Albert Einstein was prophetic when he said, "It is so strange to be so universally known, and yet so lonely."

Interestingly, not even an army of mental health workers, clinical psychologists, social workers, and therapists have been able to stem the tide of isolation. In 1950, in the USA, counselors numbered in the tens of thousands. Today, the population of mental health counselors, marriage and family counselors, and life coaches now exceeds one million. And they are not even scratching the surface in healing this terribly debilitating broken place. A disturbing study out of the University of Virginia reported a strong link between suicide and weakened social ties. People become more likely to kill themselves "when they get disconnected from one another."

For me, it is important to understand that isolation doesn't have to be just physical. Perhaps, even more often, we experience emotional, mental, and spiritual isolation while being surrounded by others. In her book, *Girl Meets God*, Lauren Winner reflects on her chosen isolation in her spiritual journey:

> I still held on to the illusion that my relationship with God could be separate from the body of people I prayed with. That it could be separate from the community. I lived with the illusion that the people next to me in the pews didn't matter, that I would go out into the desert and stand on a pole and reach up to God alone. I liked to imagine that the beliefs and recipes to get to God are enough and they exist pure and distinct from the people who enact them . . . I learned I was wrong.[15]

The impact of ISOLATION is profound, including a higher risk of dying sooner than the general population. Here are some other results of chronic loneliness:

- high blood pressure
- cardiovascular disease
- cognitive decline
- depression[16]
- reduced immunity[17]
- inflammation[18]
- poor sleep[19]
- 30-60% Increase in risk of death[20]

We are in deep trouble. You are in deep trouble because, it is likely you, too, suffer from some form of ISOLATION. No? Allow me to get personal with you for a moment. Let's take a little isolation quiz. How would you answer these questions?

- How many people know what you do for a living?
- How many people know your children's names?
- How many people have been to your home?
- How many people have eaten at your table? . . . and you at theirs?
- How many people know when you are sick and what illness you have?
- How many people would drive you to the ER if you needed help?

- How many people know the least bit about your spiritual journey?

- How many people know what gives you joy?

- How many people know what hurts your heart?

Do you see? Not many. You are more isolated than you think. You may have lots of relationships, but they are mostly secondary ones—acquaintances, connections, contacts.

This broken place is killing us.

There is a terrible amount of suffering bound up in isolation. Psychiatrists Jacqueline Olds, M.D. and Richard Schwartz, M.D noticed that "whatever other diagnostic labels might be applied to them," isolation and loneliness were the issues most deeply affecting many of their patients. In their book, *The Lonely American: Drifting Apart in the Twenty-first Century*, Olds and Schwartz called this the elephant in the room. "We began to notice how hard it was for our patients to talk about their isolation, which seemed to fill them with deep shame. Most of our patients were more comfortable saying they were depressed than saying they were lonely. Something important is changing in American relationships with one another, and that change is leaving a very large number of people very much alone."[21]

Now, my guess is that, despite all the stats and self-analysis, of all the 6 Broken Places this is the least likely to be on your radar, and the revelation that we are more okay with admitting we are depressed than that we are lonely might come as a surprise to you, particularly since neglected mental health is at the forefront of our discussions these days that arise around many societal woes. However, Olds and Schwartz found that "talking about loneliness is deeply stigmatizing; we see ourselves as a self-reliant people who do not whine about neediness. To wistfully describe how lonely he feels is simply not socially acceptable."[22] I think it comes down to the fact that depression comes with a clinical diagnosis and that helps us to treat it as something we didn't do to ourselves, whereas loneliness is viewed as simply a failure—we just aren't being strong and self-reliant enough.

What Is a Nurturer?

You, likely, haven't considered the thought that part of God's Kingdom mission on this planet is to eradicate isolation and loneliness. Oh, but it is. From the very beginning of . . . well . . . everything, healing the broken place of ISOLATION has been on God's mind.

> "The very first problem that God sought to solve, even before he took on the complications and ramifications of our sin was isolation, declaring it not good."

Consider this: This in the midst of an entire post-creation cosmos that delighted him with its very goodness.

> Then the LORD God said, "It is not good for the man to be alone. I will make a helper who is just right for him."
> —Genesis 2:18.

The Hebrew word for alone could be interpreted as "by himself or itself." And from that very early beginning of the Word of God until the end, there is an unmistakable repetition of God's desire and preference for human beings to coexist in loving community. Just as God the Father, God the Son, and God the

Holy Spirit live in perpetually loving relationship, similarly, so are human beings, made in God's image, to live with each other.

As with every other broken place, the one who most exemplified and broadcast God's concern for the broken place of ISOLATION was Jesus himself. God's agenda for love, community, and relationships is made crystal clear through Jesus' life and teaching. He set a new standard for the inclusion of women after millennia of them being treated as merely property; he physically touched the outcast ill, lame, and doomed; he welcomed children into his arms rather than shoving them to the margins; and he opened his arms even to ugly, tortured, demonized people who lived on the fringes of society.

> "This—embracing the marginalized and undesirable, showing them the same love and respect everyone else gets—is what it means to be a NURTURER of the Isolated."

And, by the way, he even sought to draw in those enemies of God whose mission was to kill and destroy him and the entire believing community. Funny, the only people he seemed to keep at arm's length were the Pharisees and teachers of the law who seemed to be isolating others!

> Hypocrites! For you shut the door of the Kingdom of Heaven in people's faces.
>
> —Matthew 23:13

Jesus' teaching was unambiguous on this subject:

> A new command I give you: Love one another. As I have loved you, so you must love one another.
>
> —John 13:34

> You must love the LORD your God with all your heart, all your soul, and all your mind. This is the first and greatest commandment. A second is equally important: Love your neighbor as yourself.
>
> —Matthew 22:37-39

Clearly, isolation is unacceptable in God's reign—God's alternate community, God's Kingdom. The leaders of the early church grasped the deep significance of eliminating isolation and pounded it into their people.

If there is one concept that most defines God's mission to draw the isolated into loving community, I would say it is that of hospitality. Three of the key early church leaders made it clear: do not permit isolation. Reach out. Love. Pull people in. Draw them into love and community!

> Practice hospitality. (Romans 12:13)
> Offer hospitality to one another without grumbling. (1 Peter 4:9)
> We ought to show hospitality. (3 John 1:8)

But I want to be sure you understand something: hospitality is a heck of a lot more than putting on a delicious spread or having clean sheets for your guests. In the first century, it was a matter of life and death. There were no Holiday Inns nor any safe highways. When people traveled, it generally took a long time through dangerous country, almost always isolated from meaningful relationships. To offer hospitality was to offer life and safety! For people unable to provide the basics of shelter and food for themselves and their families, hospitality was a lifeline.

The biblical idea of hospitality literally means to care for strangers. Hospitality was a moral and religious obligation. Hospitality was a way to pass on respect and value. Hospitality was so important that if you did not offer it to those who required it (i.e. the isolated), your reputation would be on the line. It was the glue that created a network of human interdependence—a way to administer justice to the marginalized and poor. It was one of the prime ways the Gospel spread, and it was the practice that launched the first churches.

Hospitality was the first century's tangible expression of love, and a powerful answer to the broken place of ISOLATION. It still is.

Nurturers: Healers of Isolation

If ISOLATION is the experience of feeling separated or disconnected from your environment, from loved ones, from God, then the solution would be reconnecting. While that seems easy enough . . . *You just have to go outside and say hello to someone, right?* . . . the reality is the more time you spend in isolation, the harder it is to know where to turn and the loneliness, fear of rejection, and a host of other emotional and mental challenges that stand in the way are likely to keep you from reaching out. This is why it takes people with a nurturing heart to heal the wounds and to coax people out of their isolation.

Before we move on to examples of people who are modeling the calling of NURTURING, I want to to go back to something that came up in the study from Olds and Schwartz. They found that the stigma associated with loneliness is more profound than any attached to depression, and that presents a problem. In order to reach out and nurture those who are isolated, we need to know they are *in* that situation; and, if those who are suffering are afraid to admit it, they will do everything they can to conceal it or, at the very least, not ask for help. You may not know someone is hurting until they have already taken their life or their situation has become unmanageable. If you feel

"Being a NURTURER of the Isolated also means being a hunter and a gatherer of lost souls."

your calling is to eradicate ISOLATION, it means you will likely have to go looking for those who need your help. Just as with my grandparents, many won't reach out for assistance or they'll suffer in silence until someone discovers they are living in an unacceptable state.

A nurturing soul is one that offers tenderness and understanding. Kindness propels NURTURERS to seek out people who aren't asking for help but clearly need it. So moved by the loneliness and friendlessness of others, they make time and space to open their homes and arms to others. These NURTURERS are showing us how it's done every day.

MIKE AND LIZ HENDERSON

How does a person develop a passion for hospitality? What does it take to get someone worked up about this particular broken place of ISOLATION? Mike and Liz Henderson can tell you, for these two are particularly concerned about the isolated and lonely people around them and invest large portions of their lives to drawing people into love and meaningful healing relationships.

Liz comes by this naturally. It was bred into her. Reflecting on her teen years, Liz says, "My parents taught me to look for the outsider. Some nights my dad would drop me off at the homeless shelter (to be with and care for the homeless) when I really wanted to be with my friends. They would take me to the mall and give me money to choose something for someone who needed it." Liz remembers one moment sitting in our church service as I was preaching on the concept of hospitality, and it suddenly hit her: "This is what my life is about!"

Mike and Liz also deeply care for the Isolated out of their own lonely experiences.

(Side note: as you read through this book and wrestle with which broken place might be yours to own, remember, your calling is shaped by your own experience. If your story includes significant time in a particular broken place, then you are likely to find yourself hungering to help others whose stories mimic yours.)

Back to Mike and Liz. Both of them experienced profound loneliness and isolation at points in their lives. Mike remembers the dreaded middle school years. He was a lonely young man. "I was the kid who sat alone at lunch. I believe a seed was planted then." Much later, after they married, those feelings surfaced again. Liz remembers their first year of marriage when she was in school and realized she had no one to hang out with. No one to call. No one who would call her. Then, after they moved to a new city, they realized they had no one to relate to. And they were lonely again.

But serendipitously, not long after starting to attend our church, they were asked to host a young married small group. It was then it hit Mike, "We realized that everybody lacks community!" And they threw themselves into creating an atmosphere in their groups (they've started and led several) of honesty, authentic care, and real love. Since committing themselves to this life focus, they'll tell you their calling has been magnified ten-fold!

All this was tested at one of the lowest moments of their lives when Liz had to face the horrific murder of her dearest friend while simultaneously helping her brother struggle through cancer. Liz will tell you that if it wasn't for her relationships and the community of her small groups she "would have drowned in grief." Every day "God came to the door bringing meals and our favorite things!" Today, looking back at that dark time Liz says, "No way could we ever leave this community."

So, do they have a passion for bringing healing to the isolated of this world? You bet. And they are unequivocal about their faith in the power of these relationships. "A small group of people can change the world!"

JERALD COSEY

Jerald Cosey is a man who, in his words, "attacks ISOLATION in the elderly." So determined was he to bring healing to this broken place among senior adults that in mid-life, at the height of his leadership capacities, Jerald made a radical career change and threw his whole life into ending loneliness in aging folks.

Like Mike and Liz, the roots of Jerald's calling can be found in his childhood. Jerald's parents both had died by the time he was only two years old. "My mother's mother and father raised me. So, I have always had older people in my life. And I got to see my grandma care for and love my great-grandmother until she passed away." This made a huge impression on Jerald that later bloomed into a destiny.

Most of his early career was spent in the pharmaceutical industry, but he never lost his desire to "go and visit people in nursing homes." In 2009, right after he had been downsized, over lunch I encouraged him to use his newfound extra time to pursue his desire. Not only did he begin to hang out with seniors, but he began a ministry to encourage others to join him.

Jerald looks back fondly on those early efforts at care. "The whole goal was just to care for them and be an example of love. Much of the time we would just shoot the breeze. We would just start talking about their story before they got to this nursing home, and a lot of great things came out of it. I was very proud of the diversity. Here I am, this young African American guy, and these two white men who were alive during all of the civil rights movement were sharing their life with me." The families of these men were so moved by Jerald's care for their loved ones that they considered him a part of their families and even sought his input on their lives and funerals.

The whole experience reshaped and refined Jerald's calling. After many years working in the pharmaceutical industry, Jerald took the bold step of entering into training to become an Administrator in an American Senior Community. In training, he worked *every* job in the facility, from serving food to caring for the demanding physical needs of the seniors. After a year of learning by doing, Jerald was licensed and now runs his second senior facility where he oversees 125 employees and 166 residents. Though much of his time is spent in management and oversight, he always makes time to sit down and care for his dearly loved residents. Sitting with them as they are dying, reading the Bible to them, praying with them and over them, and all the time offering his deep heart and love. Recently, a real highlight of his life has been leading an invitational Bible study in his office, and a large number of people cram into that small space to enjoy Jerald and learn about God.

Jerald loves his life. "It's been a heck of a responsibility, and it's been a great deal of joy!"

CHRIS HODGES

Chris Hodges is a NURTURER, but not in any way you might first imagine. If you saw Chris, a big burly bear of a man, your first thought might not be that he's soft and tender. But he is. He cares deeply for others and draws you in with his soft drawl and huge hug.

Much of his determined care of others comes from his own personal journey. Chris is a vet with four and a half years of active service in the Marine Corps serving in Iraq. His story, like many vets', is tough and intense, and has left him with memories he'll have to work through for the rest of his life. But it has also left him with a deep commitment to care for fellow vets, especially those who came home with physical wounds.

Not many realize how tragically isolated military vets feel, particularly those returning home with wounds. Dr. Guy Winch, PhD explains in *Psychology Today*:

> Combat veterans and prisoners of war who suffer from post traumatic stress disorder face many expected challenges when returning home and attempting to reintegrate into civilian life. But the one emotional injury we might not expect them to encounter is loneliness. A new study found many returning veterans suffer from a unique kind of loneliness, one that begins only once they are again surrounded by family and loved ones. They might have had access to deep emotional and social bonds from family and loved ones, but what they lacked—what they truly yearned for—was to feel *understood*. They wanted others to truly know what they went through, to feel what they felt as they struggled to reintegrate back into a civilian life. Yet the circumstances and experiences they suffered were so extraordinary, they felt it was practically impossible for anyone who had not been through such an experience themselves to be able to «get it»—to be able to *know*.[23]

Chris gets it, which is why he now gives a chunk of his time to the Wounded Warriors Project, an organization that provides free programs and services to meet the needs of the over 48,000 servicemen and women who have been physically injured in the recent military conflicts. Chris serves these men and women, doing something with them he dearly loves: hunting.

Chris joins with other guides taking these wounded vets out with them into the fields and forests to hunt for deer and turkey. He says most vets don't want to be there at first. But after a few days together out hunting, the guys start to open up. He'll tell you, "No one knows each other, but after 3-4 days you feel like you've known each other forever. You leave with a connection."

Chris Hodges—a giant of a man, with a tender nurturing heart, healing the broken place of ISOLATION.

JASON AND MELISSA FORCE

It was just supposed to be a quick trip to Home Depot for Jason, but upon arriving at the store, he was shocked to discover he had a stow-away emerging from under the tarp in the back of his truck. A four-year-old child from the neighborhood had secretly jumped on board for the ride. Horrified that the parents might be frantically looking for their son, Jason hurried back, only to discover that no one had even missed the kid. Jason recalls that the parents "couldn't have cared less."

That summer in Jackson, Mississippi for Jason and Melissa Force was a game-changer. The stow-away story was just one of the personal wake-up calls they received from God. All summer long, serving alongside John Perkins, Christian minister and community developer, they learned a great deal about the people they lived among—people who all struggled through dire socio-economic conditions. But, they noticed something remarkable. Some kids thrived, even in poverty, while others didn't. Melissa will tell you why: "God really convicted us that the difference was family."

Many of the kids coming from strong, loving, inter-generational families did well with life despite their circumstances. Others, like the little stow-away, struggled. Unloved. Not missed. Isolated.

From that summer on, John and Melissa dedicated their lives to creating a healthy, loving, nurturing family to as many kids as God brought their way. Their thinking: "Well, we don't have a lot. But we've got a strong family and we've got a strong relationship."

Little did they know that this decision would end up bringing dozens and dozens of children into their family over the next twenty years.

Here is just a sampling of their nurturing calling in action:

- Foster care – As many as twenty kids in and out of their home. Some of them for as little as twenty-four hours, and some longer than a year.

- Therapeutic level foster care – Taking in emergency placements with high-risk and health-challenged kids.

- Respite care – Supporting traditional foster parents who need a break or respite in dealing with difficult placements. Sometimes they cared for kids off and on for years.

- Group home – Caring for girls on probation.

- Safe Families – Temporarily hosting children for families in crisis to keep them out of foster care. Jason and Melissa have a reputation for their ability to handle the most difficult behavioral challenges.

- Adoption – Eight-year old Sierra was adopted right before she turned three.

- Their biological family – Spencer and Samuel, who have caught their parent's calling and are accepting it as their own.

What's remarkable, even beyond the scope and scale of their care and nurturing, are the obstacles they must hurdle to get up every day, let alone provide love for kids with deep needs. Melissa has, for years, struggled with inflammatory intestinal disease that led to ostomy surgery, and with complicating skin infections that required intensive wound care.

I asked them what they would say to others who shake their head in wonder at the way they live their lives. Melissa: "One of the responses I routinely get from people who hear our story is , 'That's great. I could never do that. It would break my heart.' And I always come back with something to the effect, if your heart is not breaking, you're not where God is working in the world. Instead of trusting him to give you the strength to deal with the situation, you are guarding your own heart."

Jason: "What humbles me is God says, 'Whatever you do to the least of these, you've done for me.' And that, I would say, is my motivation. Because, even though I feel like we are in a lower income bracket and we struggle sometimes, we are *so* blessed that we *have* to help. We can't sit on the couch. We just can't."

Believe me. They don't.

How to Step into Your Nurturer Calling

Remember that Jason and Melissa, Jerald, Chris, Liz and Mike all share two characteristics. On one hand they have chosen to *live brave, not safe.* Yet their forays into healing the broken place of ISOLATION have been simply one step at a time. They continue to take *the Path of Yes.*

It will take courage to engage the lonely. Fostering and adopting isolated children, for instance, are not for the faint of heart! It demands, virtually, your whole life. Investing your time and energy into seniors, while not dangerous, certainly requires an epic level of patience. Any sort of engagement with people whose lives lean toward lonely demands an others-centeredness that is just not normal in 21st century America. So, *brave, not safe!*

On the other hand, if you choose to pursue a destiny in healing ISOLATION in men, women, couples, seniors, vets, kids, or whomever, then you just have to take the next step in *the Path of Yes.* Do one thing. Then do the next. Then the next. And at some point, you may face a big decision. You may choose to offer love for the lonely at a pace or in a way that will require your very life.

But let's not get ahead of ourselves. Let's start here.

PRACTICE HOSPITALITY
This may be the single most powerful commitment you could make to heal ISOLATION. I've spoken of it in the section highlighting God's perspective on this broken place. But, let me quickly review.

Hospitality, in the early church, first-century culture was essentially about caring for strangers—making room for isolated people in your life. It was not analogous to entertaining. It was not about matching napkins or cucumber sandwiches; it was a matter of life and death. Hospitality was a moral and religious obligation.

Hospitality was a way to pass on respect and value. Hospitality was the glue that created a network of human interdependence.

Hospitality was a remedy for ISOLATION. And we need to get very good at it if we have any chance of healing loneliness.

Christine Pohl, professor at Asbury seminary, accurately captures our prevailing attitude toward it. "Christians view hospitality as a mildly pleasant activity if sufficient time is available." Hospitality feels feminine and dainty and largely unnecessary. But it is no such thing.

Hospitality is a change agent. "Hospitality means primarily the creation of free space where the stranger can enter and become a friend instead of an enemy. Hospitality is not to change people, but to offer them space where change can take place. It is not to bring men and women over to our side, but to offer freedom not disturbed by dividing lines."[24]

> Hospitality is a seed bed for love and truth.
> As we live and give witness to Jesus we are handing out seeds, not pearls, and seeds need soil in which to germinate. A meal is soil just like that. It provides a relational context in which everything you say and don't say, feel or don't feel, God's Word and snatches of gossip, gets assimilated along with the food. Nothing is abstract when you are eating a meal together. Jesus didn't drop pearls for people as clues to find their way to God. He ate meals with them. And you can do just what Jesus did.[25]

Hospitality is deeply affective and effective. It unlocks feelings. I have been fascinated with the book *Setting the Table* by wildly successful restaurateur Danny Meyer. Danny has launched many wonderful restaurants, including 11 Madison Park and Shake Shack, with the core value of hospitality. He says, "Hospitality is the sum of all the thoughtful, caring, gracious things our staff does to make you feel we are on your side when you are dining with us. Service is the technical delivery of a product. Hospitality is how the delivery of that product makes the recipient feel."[26]

Imagine a massive resurgence of hospitality in our communities and our churches! I can see it! And through it, I see ISOLATION being a thing of the past!

Now . . . how do you do hospitality? Here are some quick thoughts:

- Open your home regularly. You schedule everything else in your life from soccer games to work related events. Schedule hospitality! Set aside time to invite others into your life.

- Be more spontaneous. Lose the paranoia that your house isn't clean enough. If, to invite others into your life, you require a huge to do list or massive shopping list to prepare, something is wrong. Make hospitality simple and laid back or you will never do it.

- Open up margin in your life for hospitality. Slow down. Become sociable again. Become an essentialist. "The way of the essentialist is the relentless pursuit of less but better."[27]

- Add a chair or two around your table during the holidays and invite someone to join your family who has no one.

INTENTIONALLY ENGAGE WITH THE ISOLATED

Keep a notebook or some space in which you can record the names of lonely people you encounter. This will keep them on your radar. I know you know these things, but pay careful attention to these kinds of folks: people who live alone, those who have lost spouses or other family members, those who have just lost a job, single moms and single dads, people who have recently moved to town, college students from out-of-town, seniors, foster kids, and people with chronic illnesses . . . just to name a few. So, what can you do for them? It is not that difficult.

- Stop by their home from time to time.

- Take them out for coffee.

- Remember their important dates.

- Bless them with small gifts.

- Drop them a note.

- Give them a call.

- In church, or other social gatherings, sit with the one who is all alone.

- Students, don't let kids eat alone at school.

Again, just pay attention, listen, take a risk and jump in to their lives!

PRAY FOR THE HEALING OF ISOLATION

"Intercession is love on its knees."[28]
"While our minds are insufficient for the task of seeing to its end the explanation of intercession's power, our experience is

clear that something creative is being done when human souls take on themselves God's burden for men and in vicarious prayer throw themselves in with his sacrificial purpose."[29]

Something creative is being done when we pray! Particularly when we take on God's burden for human beings and their loneliness. Begin a prayer journal, notebook, or scrapbook that focuses on the issue of ISOLATION. List whole people groups and communities to pray for. Or, begin to list the names of anyone God brings to mind who you sense or know is facing isolation or loneliness.

Form a prayer team around an issue of isolation.

Ask your church leaders for a list of the small groups of the church and begin to pray systematically for each small group and their relationships. (Come to think of it, I've never heard of anyone doing this. But, wow, what a ministry of prayer that would be.)

No matter where you happen to be walking, pay very careful attention to the people you pass along the way. Ask God to point out to you those who are struggling with loneliness and pray for them regarding whatever God brings to mind.

And here's a little prayer tool that I've found very helpful. It's as much listening and responding as anything. Get in a quiet private place. Settle your heart. Then ask God this question: *God, will you please bring to mind right now all those who are lonely?*

He will because you asked! I guarantee names and faces will flood your head. And when they do, simply mention them back to God and ask for his intervention in their lives.

You can repeat the exercise with more specific questions, such as, *God, will you please bring to mind right now all those who have lost loved ones? God, will you please bring to mind right now seniors who need someone in their life? God, will you please bring to mind right now a single adult who has no community?* And on and on, the list of questions is endless. I promise you God will answer them and you will have more to pray for than you ever imagined!

FORM AND LEAD A SMALL GROUP

Just about every church I know has some form of small groups. They call them life groups, care groups, home groups, or house churches. And they serve all kinds of purposes—Bible study, prayer for each other, communal meals, just hanging out, or "doing life together."

I wonder about small groups. I'm just being honest, but it seems to me that I hear less and less enthusiastic commitment to small groups. I have a theory about this. I think small groups just cost too much these days. No, not money, but the greater, more precious currency: time. The small group Penny and I had been a part of for years and years, just recently decided to end our formal gatherings primarily because we just couldn't seem to get it together. It was a rare night when every member of the group could gather. Other commitments outweighed the group, pure and simple.

I know there are other reasons small group commitment may be waning. But, cutting to the chase, I believe what we have is an essentialism problem. Greg McKeown suggests we are no longer living by design but by default.[30] We believe we can fit it all in. We are falling into the undisciplined pursuit of more.[31] And, the preponderance of choice has overwhelmed our ability to manage it.[32]

We have a big essentialism problem and one of the causalities is small group participation.

That said, I still believe in the vision of small groups. It is still one of the best solutions to isolation. Done well, small groups provide the kind of intimacy we all need to deal with our growing loneliness.

Let's return to Mike and Liz Henderson. Here's what they are doing that continues to make their small groups vibrant and personally relevant:

- They throw themselves into creating an atmosphere in their groups of honesty, authentic care, and real love.

- Their groups "do life together"—they celebrate, grieve, etc.

- They serve together—loving on foster kids, seniors, and others. Mike and Liz help them keep the focus always on "the other."

- They put a premium on affirming one another often and well. "We're not going to wait until we die. We're going to tell each other what we admire about them. We want affirmation!"

- They show up at the most important times.

- And they tell their group to always consider inviting a new couple. "There's always room at the table."

In a word, Mike and Liz are intentional with their small groups. And that is exactly what it will take from us all if we intend to heal isolation through small group engagement.

INTENTIONALLY SEEK OUT SENIORS

We'd do well to follow the lead of Jerald Cosey and "attack

isolation in seniors." Here are several ways to engage our elderly friends and family who spend so much of their time alone.

First, pay attention to the seniors in your sphere of influence who are falling through the relational cracks. Take an inventory of the people who are your physical neighbors. Who is alone? Look in the seats of your congregation as they gather. Who is sitting by themselves? Do you notice seniors at the gym who regularly are by themselves? Again . . . just pay attention. You know how once you look into buying a certain type of car you see them everywhere? Well, the same will happen if you intentionally look for the lost and lonely.

Another, more organized way to hang out with lonely seniors is to partner with organizations whose mission is to do just that and meet their needs. Meals on Wheels comes to mind. Since the 1940s in post-war Great Britain, they have been serving the needs of the hungry and lonely seniors of our world. Volunteer opportunities abound!

And I hope some of you who are passionate about this broken place of ISOLATION will determine to make it your mission to simply hang out with seniors who are institutionalized. Maybe start with your own family! And maybe include your whole family! Imagine the joy of an aging adult whose world has been shrinking for years, to suddenly have people who listen and care and love.

PROVIDE CARE FOR ISOLATED KIDS

The decision to provide love and care for isolated kids can certainly run the gamut of commitment. On one end of the spectrum, you could simply volunteer with your church's student ministry or partner with other organizations that invest in kids. Organizations like Big Brothers and Big Sisters of America do an incredible job of touching the lives of lonely kids. I know I'm a broken record, but simply pay attention and do your homework. There are dozens of mission organizations right in your area who are desperate for people like you to love on kids!

The next step, perhaps, in intensity and time commitment would be to become a foster parent. Every year, a quarter of a million children come into foster care in this country. There aren't enough families to take them in, so a good number end up in group homes. Foster parents play a critical role in helping isolated kids. Fostering is not for the faint of heart. It is obviously intense and time consuming, but it could help end loneliness and isolation for generations!

One organization that has done a phenomenal job of providing an alternative to fostering is Safe Families for Children. Located in seventy cities across the United States, United Kingdom, Canada and beyond, Safe Families is motivated by compassion to keep children safe and out of foster care. Safe Families create extended family-like support for desperate families through a community of devoted volunteers who are motivated by faith to keep children safe and keep families intact. They're well worth your investigation if you feel the call to care for isolated kids.

Finally, there is adoption. This is clearly a lifetime calling and not to be entered into without a sense of destiny. There are over 160 million orphans in the world. The number of lonely kids is staggering. Twenty thousand kids age out of foster care every year. Perhaps the hand of God is on your life to take this huge leap?

ENGAGE YOUR COMPANY IN COMMUNITY WORK

I love the creative passionate sense of corporate social responsibility that Danny Meyer has bred into his group of restaurants.

> One of the most significant benefits we offer our employees is the opportunity to work for a company that stands for something well beyond serving food in a comfortable environment. I make it very clear to all new employees that they've joined a company that chooses to take an active interest in its community and that we rely on members of our staff to step up and participate as citizens within that culture.[33]

One of the many programs he's instituted (and his employees love) is their Hospice Dinner program at Beth Israel hospital. Every Tuesday and Wednesday one of their restaurants prepares twenty dinners for the hospice unit, and volunteers from the restaurant staff deliver and serve them. These often lonely people and families get to not only enjoy some spectacular food, but they are noticed and loved. Danny says, "It's impossible for anyone on our team to serve at the hospice program and not return to work with a far deeper understanding of the true meaning and impact of life and hospitality."[34] And, Danny maintains that this and the other community care activities in which they engage strengthen their love and care for each other in the process.

What can your company do to end ISOLATION? Have you thought about how your company's mission intersects with the mission of God?

You, Again

Maybe, just maybe, you have been placed here on this planet to be the answer to somebody's deep loneliness. Look, it doesn't have to be complicated. You have this uncanny knack for creating warm and inviting environments, don't you? Your heart is no Grinch's heart . . . it is wide and open to all people. This is how God made you, no? Then get on it.

Begin to heal this broken place of ISOLATION in big and little ways. And take somebody with you. How about your whole family? There is a kid out there with no family of her own. Find her. Bring her in. Love on her. With the help of God, heal her broken heart. Or rally a group of people together in community. Or start a ministry to seniors. Or, whatever . . .

Get in this game. Live your calling as a NURTURER and make the world a lot less lonely.

CHAPTER 4
HEALERS

"It hurts, but that's okay . . . I'm used to it."
—author unknown

Not long ago I was sitting in our weekly staff prayer meeting with a group of young guys reflecting on life and the importance of strong community. In the middle of the conversation one young man said this: "Yeah, if I had stayed in my former job I would have put a bullet in my brain." At first I thought he was making some exaggerated claim of frustration with his job, but he wasn't. He was speaking honestly. Everyone in the group nodded because they knew he was not speaking in hyperbole. I was shocked. I had no idea. He seemed like such a cool, put-together guy. But apparently his mental health had degenerated to the point of thoughts of suicide. His pain was so deep from a broken relationship, coupled with a community that didn't seem to want to help, that the idea of being dead felt better than being alive. Joining our staff and forming new community literally saved his life.

I wish this was unusual. I wish this level of pain was an anomaly. But it is not. This level of pain is chronic. It is widespread. It is pervasive. It is insidious. And it is growing.

Recently, *New York Times Magazine* published an article that received a great deal of attention. The article tells the story of Jake whose parents sent him to a therapist in middle school when he was too scared to sleep in his own room. But this was only the beginning.

Jake had begun refusing to go to school and simply curled up in the fetal position on the floor, crying, "I just can't take it!" He began suffering physical symptoms as well, developing stomach pains and migraines. "All of a sudden I couldn't do anything," he said. "I was so afraid."

Jake's parents took him to his primary-care physician, who prescribed Prozac—the first of many medications prescribed to Jake over the next year, some of which made a bad situation worse. The article reports, "An increased dosage made Jake 'much more excited, acting strangely and almost manic.' A few weeks later, Jake locked himself in a bathroom at home and tried to drown himself in the bathtub."

Jake was hospitalized for four days, but nothing improved, and he sank deeper into hopelessness and depression. During spring break in 2016, his father reported a day when they saw him return to normal, but a week later, Jake threatened suicide again. His younger siblings were terrified. His mother described it as "the depth of hell."[35]

"The depth of hell." Now that is pain.

The National Institute of Mental Health estimates that anxiety disorders affect 18.1% of adults in the United States (approximately 40 million adults between the ages of 18 to 54) with only roughly 40% receiving treatment of any kind. Nearly 1 out of 10 Americans suffers from some form of depression (350 million world-wide). Martin Seligman, head of the American Psychological Association, believes that the United States is in the throes of an epidemic of clinical depression. He says an American today is significantly more likely to suffer clinical depression at some point in his or her life than at any other time in the past hundred years.[36]

About a year ago I was invited by our Student Ministry Team to attend a special event they hosted for our high school students where time would be set aside to pray over any of the kids who requested it. When the time came, and the floor was opened to them, kids came streaming to us. As expected, there were a few who asked for prayer for physical pain or relationship problems, but the vast majority of the kids came weeping . . . sobbing . . . to us with severe chronic issues of anxiety—debilitating, sleep-depriving, health-destroying anxiety. I was stunned at the intensity and volume of the problem. According to an article in *Psychology Today*, the average high school kid of today has the same level of anxiety as the average institutionalized psychiatric patient in the early 1950s.[37] I believe it.

Mental illness has become so pervasive in the suburbs of Indianapolis that one of our local mayors, Scott Fadness, in his first term as mayor of Fishers, Indiana, determined to launch a wide-ranging initiative to call attention to the pain and devastating ramifications of mental illness.

The mental health initiative was started in Fishers a year ago, after Fadness had a ride-along with a police officer and asked him what calls concerned him the most. "Well, it's IDs." Fadness asked him, "What? Are you talking about a driver's license?" The officer said, "No, it's immediate detentions." Fadness says, "I thought, *What do those mean?*, and the officer replied, 'It's when we get taken to a call and someone is in such duress that they are going to do immediate harm to themselves or someone else.'"

Fadness says he started looking at the data. "And, every Monday I read these intelligence reports that literally say . . . five people tried to commit suicide last week, or seven people .

.. two were successful . . . ages ranging from nine years old to seventy years old." This spurred him on to create a task force of school, health, public safety, and city leaders to explore mental health issues. Fadness says that in the past year the group has clearly identified stigma as a barrier to care. "In Fishers, these are people living in quiet despair; you wouldn't know that they have depression—the woman who shoots herself on Tuesday night, that day probably went to work."

After a year-long assessment, the Fishers Mental Health Task Force is now working to coordinate care, increase training, and reduce stigma. National statistics show that about a quarter of Americans suffer from mental illness in a given year, but around half of those people will not seek treatment, in part, because of stigma. And that last part— reducing stigma—is the key focus that is trending across the country right now.

Mayor Fadness says about one in five residents suffer from a mental health condition, and he doesn't believe his city is unique. "Every community, I don't care what demographic, is dealing with this issue today, or not dealing with it, but it's still there."[38]

This broken place of PAIN, and mental illness in particular, is not simply an individual problem. This is not just about a person suffering in the tortured recesses of their minds . . . although it is that. This pain is setting off a tsunami of shootings—mass murder and mayhem that is bringing our nation to its knees. I wrestled with which broken place they fit under. PAIN? INJUSTICE? HATRED? I could even make the argument that they fit under SEPARATION. In the end, they really are grotesque illustrations of both PAIN and HATRED. Some of them clearly are the result of deranged, mentally sick people given access to military-style weaponry. As I type these words right now, law enforcement officials and community leaders are still investigating three mass murders in the last month—90 dead, nearly 600 injured. This is the grim tally of just one month in the life of our country, and I fear, no matter when you read this, there will be some place in America where there is a similar story in current news. The perpetrators are sick, sick people. And our nation is a sick, sick place to live. Utterly broken with pain.

And that's just mental or emotional pain. What of physical pain?

I am all too familiar with the physical sort of pain. At times it feels as though my wife and I are personally funding the bulk of the American health system. Okay, that's hyperbole. But it sure feels true. In the last several years, between the two of us we have consulted with an internist, otolaryngologist, rheumatologist, allergist, several gastroenterologists, a urologist, numerous radiologists, an ER doctor, a specialist in pain management, a physical therapist, a doctor of Functional Medicine, a surgeon, a doctor of Integrative Medicine, and a dentist.

Both of us, just like you and many, many others in pain, have suffered. I'm not complaining (really, I'm not), just reflecting on the fact that if Penny and I, who, despite how it sounds, are relatively healthy, imagine the countless millions who daily find it hard to get out of bed, or sleep, or simply function due to chronic physical pain.

Pain. Just. Is.

According to the National Center for Health Statistics (2006), approximately 76.2 million—one in every four Americans—have suffered from pain that lasts longer than twenty-four hours, and millions more suffer from acute pain. And it gets worse. A terrible result of all this pain is a crisis the likes of which this nation and the world has never dealt with before—an opioid abuse epidemic.

The U.S. Department of Health and Human Services has captured the stunning data we now face. There are 12.5 million people now misusing prescription opioids. That number is growing by over two million per year as new abusers emerge. Over 15,000 people per year are dying from overdoses of prescribed opioids. Deaths from prescription opioids— drugs like oxycodone, hydrocodone, and methadone—have more than quadrupled since 1999, and the Center for Disease Control reports that overdoses from prescription opioids are a driving factor in the significant increase in opioid overdose deaths. The amount of prescription opioids sold to pharmacies, hospitals, and doctors' offices nearly quadrupled from 1999 to 2010, yet there had not been an overall change in the amount of pain that Americans reported.[39]

Pain is all around us and in us. It is endemic to the human condition. The fact is, we live in a world of broken bodies, minds, and spirits. Pain is clearly and obviously one of the 6 Broken Places of the world. I don't have to convince anybody of that truth. But before we move on and examine the healing that must occur and who can step into the gap to provide it, I must touch on one more area of pain that might make you scratch your head or, quite possibly, cause you to walk away from this book.

I'm going to call this dark pain.

This is the kind of pain that does not originate from within but is imposed on us from outside. This kind of pain comes from forces outside of our control. And by forces, I mean malevolent beings bent on our harassment and destruction. And—putting a finer point on it—by malevolent beings, I mean Satan and his demons. Still with me?

I do not have stats, but I have real, honest to goodness experiences with many tortured souls—men and women, boys and girls debilitated with the stuff of nightmares and creepy oppression—people terrorized by real, but spiritual, entities that so bedevil them that they end up with severe mental illness, physical illness, or both.

I'm talking about people who are demonized—under the influence of a demon. Talk about pain! Warning: I am about to creep you out.

There was the woman manifesting superhuman strength, having to be held down by three men, threatening me with harm in a deep, growling voice that wasn't hers. There was the teen who made a crazy agreement with the devil and spent months fighting off suicidal thoughts as a result. There was the man who invited evil to invade his life and instantly "felt a thousand fingers pushing into his body," and the woman who heard constant voices over her shoulder condemning and mocking her, driving her to despair. I have watched people's bodies physically contorted, have personally felt waves of dark terror fill a room as I've prayed over demonized people, and have wept as people poured out disgusting dreams and images they experience regularly.

And I'm not even telling you the *really* weird stories. Yes, many of these stories have roots in mental illness; but I've gotta tell you, that doesn't explain it all. Seriously, there are forces outside of us bent on our destruction.

So, again . . . pain. Lots of pain. It is a broken place . . . deep and dark.

Over the last few years, as I have processed my own pain (prayed, consulted, wept, worried, and researched), I have found myself much more sensitive to the brokenness of PAIN in the people of my congregation, community, and life. I listen harder, hug longer, and pray way more fervently than ever for people in pain.

The apostle Paul, early Christian missionary and prophet, succinctly captured the world's agony when he wrote, "We long for our bodies to be released from suffering."

This verse serves as a summary reflection on all the 6 Broken Places. Early in his letter written to first-century Christians living in Rome, Paul said, "For we know that all creation has been groaning as in the pains of childbirth right up to the present time. And we also groan . . . for we long for our bodies to be released from sin and suffering." (Romans 8:22-23)

Groaning. I'm not sure any one word states the obvious as much as that. Groaning is an onomatopoeia—a word that resembles or suggests the sound that it describes. It sounds like its cousin word moaning. We do a lot of that, don't we?

The Bible is unsparing in its honest expression of our physical, emotional, and mental pain. Right from the get-go God predicted pain would be a constant nemesis . . . and by the way, again, it is our own fault.

> God said to the woman, "I will sharpen the pain of your pregnancy, and in pain you will give birth. And you will desire to control your husband, but he will rule over you." And to the

man he said, "Since you listened to your wife and ate from the tree whose fruit I commanded you not to eat, the ground is cursed because of you.

"All your life you will struggle to scratch a living from it. It will grow thorns and thistles for you, though you will eat of its grains. By the sweat of your brow will you have food to eat until you return to the ground from which you were made. For you were made from dust, and to dust you will return.'" (Genesis 3:16-19)

That divine prophecy is loaded with agony—relational, physical, and emotional—culminating with the ultimate pain of death.

On and on it goes throughout the story of the people of God. Pain of all sorts. Noah's drunken stupor, Sarah's infertility, Jacob's limp, the misery of God's people in captivity, Moses' self-loathing, Ruth's deep loss, and David's horror. But, nowhere is pain more poignant than in the story of the great sufferer of all time: Job.

> Why is life given to those with no future,
> those God has surrounded with difficulties?
> I cannot eat for sighing; my groans pour out like water.
> What I always feared has happened to me.
> What I dreaded has come true.
> I have no peace, no quietness.
> I have no rest; only trouble comes.
>
> —Job 3:23-26

We hurt. We groan. We moan. We agonize. It is our lot. Leave it to Jesus himself to summarize it succinctly when he said,

"Here on earth you will have many trials and sorrows." (John 16:33) Blood, sweat, tears, trauma, debilitating pain. He felt it all.

What Is a Healer?

Clearly PAIN is one of the 6 Broken Places of this world. Yet, while horrible, not unsolvable; while tragic, not a forgone conclusion. In perhaps God's most revelatory glimpse of a world in which pain is lessened—a picture of a hopeful future—a man named John was given a peculiar daydream by God.

Don't miss this: "He will wipe every tear from their eyes. There will be no more death or mourning or crying or pain, for the old order of things has passed away." (Revelation 21:4)

For years I believed this was simply our future hope—that one day our pain would be eradicated, our tears dried, our groaning over when we step on to the other shore of Heaven. In other words, when we die. But now I understand more clearly that God's promise of healing from pain is also something we can experience right here, right now, because the Kingdom of God is "at hand"! It is graspable, present, and quite possible.

"God's promise of healing from pain is also something we can experience right here, right now, because the Kingdom of God is "at hand"! It is graspable, present, and quite possible."

Jesus is the best model for the amazing healing possibilities of the Kingdom. Numerous passages of Scripture inform us that just about everywhere Jesus went he healed.

...he healed every disease and sickness among the people.

—Matthew 4:23

But He also commanded his followers to follow suit:

> "I tell you the truth, anyone who believes in me
> will do the same works I have done, and even
> greater works, because I am going to be with
> the Father. You can ask for anything in my
> name, and I will do it, so that the Son can bring
> glory to the Father. Yes, ask me for anything in
> my name, and I will do it!"
>
> —John 14:12-14

And they did!

> The apostles performed many miraculous signs
> and wonders among the people. People brought
> the sick into the streets and laid them on beds
> and mats so that at least Peter's shadow might
> fall on some of them as he passed by. Crowds
> gathered bringing their sick and all of them
> were healed.
>
> —Acts 5:12-15

I would contend that this expectation has been handed down over the centuries to every new generation of Christ followers. Late in the first century, something quite remarkable happened among followers of Jesus. Two tragic epidemics broke out in the Middle East that took the lives of vast portions of the population. There was world-wide panic. Bodies, some still alive, were tossed into the road, heaped on top of each other. People died with no care whatsoever given to them.

In the midst of these deadly plagues, a group of people arose who determined it was their responsibility to do something about the tragedy unfolding around them. Followers of Christ, some very new to their faith, moved into the streets and began to take care of the sick and dying. They believed they had a mandate from Jesus himself to put themselves at grave risk and provide help for the suffering.

Dionysius, the third century bishop of Alexandria, reflected on this radical care. "Heedless of the danger they took charge of the sick, attending to their every need. And with them departed this life serenely happy, for they were infected by others with the disease, drawing on themselves the sickness of their neighbors, and cheerfully accepting their pain."[40]

It was these Christians of the Roman Empire who began to change society's attitude to the sick, disabled and dying. Much of what we know today as health care including doctors, clinics, and hospitals began with these brave acts of followers of Jesus.

Healing is our mandate. Perhaps, we have even more capabilities to bring healing into broken bodies, minds, and spirits than we are even aware. Healing is very much within our power.

Healers of Pain

It will take an army of praying, caring, embracing, listening, diagnosing, and loving people to bring healing to this broken place. Of course, we need health professionals who follow their calling as followers of Jesus, but we need everyday folk who ache with those who suffer and are willing to invest the time to love them well.

And like our first century predecessors who bravely exposed themselves to real and perceived danger caring for those in pain, we must do the same. An inspiring, albeit horrifying, example is that of Dr. Kent Brantly who contracted the ebola virus while serving with Samaritan's Purse in Liberia in 2014. His harrowing story has been captured in a documentary *Facing Darkness*. Reflecting on the film, Dr. Brantly offered this: "It's a message that our country and the church needs to hear right now: to act out of love instead of reacting out of fear. It doesn't mean you don't feel afraid, but you choose to act out of love anyway."[41]

No, the average person will not have to face such rare and deadly diseases as they seek to heal pain in hurting people. But coming alongside folks suffering with any one of a number of mental illnesses, for instance, will take significant courage. There is risk in caring for those burdened with an addiction to substance abuse. It can be a huge burden, seeking to bring healing to those saddled not only with deep pain but crushing poverty. It can be life draining to patiently sit with the chronically ill. And it can be downright dangerous ministering to those whose pain comes from dark sources, the spiritual world.

But, I know you. You who are touched with this calling. You who feel it deep within. You who are driven by this destiny to bring healing to pain. The warnings and stories do not dissuade you one bit. They spur you on!

Here, then, are some of your comrades. Listen to the stories of a few people I admire who are carrying on the centuries-old Christian tradition of caring for those suffering and in pain.

DR. CHARLIE KELLEY

It is likely that Charlie's call to be a doctor was born on his fifteenth birthday when he helplessly watched his father pass away from a heart attack. "There was no medical response." That's how he described the moment. And now, over seventy years later, he realizes that frustration gave rise to a passion to provide a response to thousands of people in pain and facing suffering.

Dr. Charlie Kelley and his wife Lorraine both graduated from medical school in 1964. Charlie is most certainly not what I would consider to be a "typical" doctor. From the beginning of living out his calling, he has been driven by a passion to care for the poor—those he describes as folks who "had no options." This led them to a two-year stint in the Peace Corps in Afghanistan. As he established his Internal Medicine practice, he never lost sight of that internal drive to make sure that the "poor received the best possible care."

He helped spearhead the development of the first urban health clinic in the city of Indianapolis, this during the tumultuous late 1960s—a time of great unrest in America. There were no clinics for the marginalized and poor, let alone any that would model Charlie's dream of a "one-class system of care," where the rich would sit with the poor in the very same waiting room. But he made it happen.

As Charlie recalled those early days of living out his calling, he teared up, remembering the non-negotiable commitment he had for dressing up in a coat and tie as he cared for the poor. He wanted all of his patients to be able to say with pride, "That's my doctor!" Charlie told me, "My mission was to demonstrate the value of personhood in the midst of suffering, even to those who were the bane of society."

Charlie continued to work in health clinics even after retirement, driven by his love of God and people, especially those he referred to as "the undesirables," such as those whose toenails had curled around the front of their toes due to neglect. When he treated those folks, he would patiently trim their nails and callouses. He told me that was one of his most enjoyable moments. "I still love doing that; you just have to wear glasses and close your mouth as you do it!"

VICTORIA WILBURN

Like just about everyone else I've interviewed for this book, Victoria Wilburn first got a hint of her calling very early in life, maybe as early as five years old! Most of her childhood was spent in therapy from a struggle with scoliosis. The love and care from her own therapists sparked an interest in her to become a health professional, which led all the way to Boston University where she graduated with a degree in Occupational Therapy.

As an Occupational Therapist, Victoria is driven to help people bring back normalcy into their lives wracked with suffering and pain. She says, "I love helping people do the little things we take for granted, even as small a thing as brushing their teeth." It is this passion and philosophy of people care she now passes on to her students at Indiana University/Purdue University (IUPUI) where she teaches as an assistant professor and Doctor of Health Science.

She is committed to seeing a new generation of young men and women move into the broken place of PAIN and suffering with compassion and care. And her calling has expanded as well, touching on issues of INJUSTICE along with PAIN. One day not long ago, she felt as if God was giving her an expanded vision to provide hope and healing for people facing homelessness along with addictions and depression. She began to explore a new kind of care called Narrative Medicine, that helps people to know and to tell their own story. As she has practiced this with the marginalized people God brought her way, she has begun to see that their minds and bodies actually decrease in pain and they are able to cope with their depression.

This new dimension of healing has led her and a friend to create the non-profit Art of Healing. Working with a number of private and government organizations, Vic and Sally have been empowering those who have no voice to speak their story, even through innovative work using theater. The love, care, and healing Vic received as a child she now passes on to the voiceless, the broken, and the suffering. She knows why she is here!

SHARON STOHLER

Sharon also feels called to address pain and suffering in people's lives. But her methods might seem more unconventional. Sharon has the spiritual gift of healing. Meaning, she lays hands on hurting people and prays for them to receive the healing touch of God. And many of them do!

Sharon explains how she came to this place of offering divine healing prayer for people:

"The conviction to minister to people in the broken place of PAIN grew from two sources: a season of experiencing my own deep emotional pain and a supernatural encounter with the Holy Spirit.

"Circumstances in our family caused debilitating wounds to grow to a point where it was a challenge to even worship. My entire personality had disappeared, and simply getting through the day was often my only goal. With the help of family, friends, and therapists, the fog of my life eventually lifted, until one day I woke up and realized I had been healed.

"Shortly after that realization, I was sitting in a worship service and my arms began to tingle and my palms started to sweat. A few months earlier, I heard a testimony of a woman who knew she was being prompted by the Spirit to heal whenever her palms would sweat. Instinctively, I knew these sensations were indicators for me to seek out someone who needed healing prayer. Although I never ended up praying for a specific person for healing that day, it was the occasion when the Lord got my attention about how He wanted to use me. Over the course of the next few months, four different strangers prophesied over me something related to healing. There was no need for neon signs. The Lord had spoken.

"At first, I was very hesitant to admit that I had been given a gift of healing. Even so, I became fascinated with the topic, reading several books and attending conferences on the subject. Within a few months, my compassion for people experiencing physical and emotional pain increased. Laying hands on people to pray for healing had once seemed frightening, but quickly changed to a delight. When I began to pray for people in pain, while partnering with the Holy Spirit to accomplish the plans of Jesus, I discovered a fresh joy and passion I never knew before. The true gift was revealed in the giving."

DR. JIM MEACHAM

Jim will tell you that at one point in his life he had "everything"—a successful career as an endocrinologist with a grateful group of patients who trusted him at Indiana

University Health. And, on top of that, an office with a gorgeous view where he could sit and watch the squirrels. He gave all of that up to enter the demanding and challenging world of outpatient addiction medicine.

Why? Why leave the comfort, the satisfaction, the fine facilities, and the squirrels? Because Dr. Jim Meacham determined that his God-given destiny lay in bringing healing to the broken place of PAIN, specifically among those overwhelmed by their battle with addiction.

His journey into that specific calling was shaped over the course of his entire life. "Throughout my life, my Dad was what might be called a 'functional alcoholic'; quite dysfunctional actually, but he worked every day and provided for the family. He was a great guy, but could not put down the bottle for anything but his work. He committed suicide in March 2000. His father was similarly affected by alcohol addiction. Multiple other close family members of mine have had substance use disorders. By God's grace, those still alive are, after years of struggle, all in recovery."

But over the last fifteen years or so, Jim's journey became more of a saga. Through a number of profound experiences and relationships, God showed Jim that his family's struggle would become his driving passion.

In 2004, one of his family members entered an addiction treatment center. Jim says, "It was at that time that I began to connect with some of the support services there. It was those connections that gave me a front row seat in the addiction community." He was so moved by the love and care of the doctors and staff that he began volunteering at the addiction center and then pulled others into serving with him, specifically a small group of young adults from our church. He invited these suburban young people to simply sit down with young adults from the treatment center and have conversations. It was life-changing for both groups of young men and women and for Jim. In time, Jim felt led to craft a church-based young adult recovery group that continues to offer a safe environment for recovery in Jesus' name.

I'll let him tell you in his own words what happened in Toronto while he was ministering with an organization that loves and cares for street people and how this experience "wrecked" him for good.

"My first day in Toronto I wondered, What in the hell am I doing here? I'm a 50-something endocrinologist from the suburbs. Why am I here? Then God punched me in the nose. In the parking lot, I come across a guy laying under a car like he'd been hit by it, but he's just trying to find some shade. As I walk by him, he starts having grand mal seizures and banging his head on the pavement. He's seizing so bad, I put my pack under his head and turned it to the side so if he threw up, he wouldn't aspirate. I'm doing what I knew to do as a doctor, but I had nothing. The day before, I was in an environment where I could have put in an IV. I could have given him medicine. I could have intubated his airway. Yet there he was in my hands, turning blue and, again, I had nothing. It was then God said to me, 'You don't need anything. I'm here. You can care for the least of these in the most unusual environments.'"

Through Jim's trip to Haiti, his calling was secured: "We were in a tent that is like 100 degrees, maybe hotter. It was a pretty miserable experience. When we get there at nine o'clock in the morning, there's already 100 people to be seen. I come out of suburban medical practice where I'm seeing 15-20 people a day; so, I'm sitting there, and this woman comes, and she's got these huge sunglasses sitting crooked on her face and I wondered why that was. She takes her sunglasses down and this big tumor is growing out of her face. And I'm sitting there and I don't know what to do. I don't have CT scan, I got no medicine, I don't even have a bandage to put on. I'm just sitting there and I've got nothing. So, I do what I can. I get some ointments, I put a dressing over it."

Looking back on his life and these experiences, Jim says, "It all starts from a position of being powerless. I got nothing. I've been shown over and over again that I've got nothing for the addiction community except for what God has shown me, and now he wants to use it. All these little stories, in my head, are tied together. They are inseparable."

In late 2015, Jim responded to the call of God on his life and entered the world of addiction medicine. He eventually found his way to an outpatient addiction center in Indianapolis called Clean Slate where he threw himself into the tragic and mushrooming opioid epidemic.

Jim says, "It feels surreal, but this is where my people are. This is where the battle is taking place. This is the great evil of our day. But, this is where I'm supposed to be." And he'll tell you, "I've still got nothing."

(Side note: In an amazing after-story, Jim eventually found a way and the means to bring Luvonna, the woman with the tumor, to the States and arranged for a hospital and doctors to have her tumor removed.)

How to Step into Your Healer Calling

Does the agony of others aggravate you? Does mental illness always make your own heart hurt? Does the tragedy faced by others persistently agitate you? If so, I'll bet your calling lies somewhere within this broken place of PAIN.

I have a good number of friends who have followed their heart into professional healthcare. Doctors, nurses, therapists, and caregivers of all kinds knew they had no choice but to follow this path. But note that even Drs. Kelley and Meacham, in paying attention to God's call, continued to say "yes" as they honed their destiny among the poor and addicted. The point . . . always keep saying yes! And take the next step. Those steps, whether as professional caregivers or simply caring friends will eventually lead you to the place of courage. You will, in due time, be forced to *live brave, not safe*. For bringing healing to desperate pain requires great nerve.

But again, let's not get ahead of ourselves. One step of love at a time. One act of care. One prayer of passion. One moment of patience.

In time, yes, you will encounter a person so full of pain that it will require all that you have within you to face it. But by then, having become an expert in the path of yes, you will love them like a trooper. You will realize again that you were made for this. And you will know you have a why to live for!

VOLUNTEER AT A HOSPITAL

Years ago, I served in an ER as a volunteer orderly. I helped unload ambulances, cleaned up exam rooms, and got lunch for the doctors. It is why I studied pre-med in college for a while, though obviously went a different way. It was an experience that shaped me profoundly! I doubt that today's hospitals would offer such an intense opportunity, but there are plenty of other ways for you to offer care to those in pain.

My daughter, Lucy, for instance, while living in Cincinnati realized she was, in her words, getting "swallowed up in my own bubble." She wanted to "connect to a broader purpose." Because she has always had a passion for kids, she looked into volunteering at Cincinnati Children's Hospital. There she discovered a very cool way to bring hope and healing to kids and their parents who were suffering and in pain. She served as a Child Life Specialist.

Once a week after work, she would don scrubs or even full protective gear and enter kids' hospital rooms to offer a measure of peace or fun or rest for the kids or their parents. She would bring a variety of toys and games to entertain them and help them get their minds off of their pain or the long waiting for medical diagnosis and care. Many times, she would end up sitting with or holding a child who had no parent to be with them. Check out your local hospital. I'm guessing there are plenty of ways you can help too!

JUST BE THERE

In theory, this idea of being there is quite easy. Just hang out with someone who is suffering. No, you don't have to have answers or even necessarily talk. Just be there. Visit them in their home or in the hospital. Sit with them during chemo or while they wait for testing.

Another especially important area is grief care. If you pursue a calling here, it might be as simple as working with your church and pastor to provide comfort and aid to families who are having to go through the process of burying a loved one. We have some folks at our church who have dedicated themselves to this and, believe me, it makes a huge difference in the lives of those suffering with grief.

Walking alongside someone who is dying or who has experienced the death of a dear loved one is a calling that can feel daunting. It can be extremely uncomfortable. What do I say?

Do they want to be left alone? What if I do something to make it worse? These are the thoughts we all struggle with. But, once again, the key is presence—being there—showing up. Your presence might provide the healing needed in a time of great transition.

> "The key is presence—being there—showing up. Your presence might provide the healing needed in a time of great transition."

SERVE IN A RECOVERY COMMUNITY

A recovery community is a network of individuals who share the common goal of lifelong sobriety and offer support and fellowship to their peers. Those in recovery struggle with multi-layered pain, and many are truly feeling it for possibly the first time in their lives. Just about any recovery community from 12-Step Programs to half-way houses to sober living facilities would appreciate any loving investment you could offer!

PARTNER WITH HEALING ORGANIZATIONS

Just about any type of illness, whether physical or mental, has an army of people, both professional and volunteer, giving themselves to its healing. A simple Google search of websites focusing on cancer or Alzheimer's or anxiety disorders or depression will reveal countless ways for you to serve those in pain. Whether you are offering fund-raising support for the organization, getting involved in education and awareness, or just serving those seeking support through the organization, there is a place for you and your gifts.

WORK WITH HEALTH CLINICS

Again, the options here are many. I have observed clinics, both local and international, doing incredible Kingdom work among the marginalized. And I have been moved by volunteers who have thrown themselves into working alongside the health professionals who live life pursuing their destiny in alleviating and healing suffering.

On one end of the spectrum of involvement are the folks who show up to wash floors and paint walls; on the other end are the people who throw themselves headlong into the work of being the hands and feet of Jesus among the bloody and bruised.

Just the other day, I sat stunned and weeping, hearing the story of Dr. Samer Attar, an American-born orthopedic surgeon who, as a part of the Syrian American Medical Society, has travelled to the middle of the Syrian battlefield to bring hope and healing to those crushed by the war. He said in an interview on 60 Minutes, "You work with the understanding that you might find yourself dead, or . . . or crippled, or dismembered on the floor next to the people you're trying to save. Because the bombs would land so close they'd . . . they'd knock you off your feet."[42]

Feel the tug just reading that? You are needed, whether it's to scrub a floor, set a broken bone, or hold a quivering hand.

PRAY FOR HEALING

Why not start a prayer journal or notebook or scrapbook centered on those suffering and in pain? Form a prayer team around the topic or around a community beset with pain. Become a prayer warrior for any one of the thousands of clinics providing health care for the poor. You can focus your prayers on the mental health of your city. Or just sit and wait on God to bring to your mind those who are suffering. If you do, he will.

Create a movement of healing prayer in your church. Some call them Healing Rooms. We call them Hope Rooms—places for unhurried, Spirit-inspired prayer for the broken and suffering. Build them and people will come to live out their destiny and the command of Jesus to heal the sick! Remember this: The weapons we fight with are not the weapons of the world. On the contrary, they have divine power to demolish strongholds. (See 2 Cor. 10:4)

You, Again

One of the great joys of writing this book has been doing the interviews with the folks I've highlighted as healers of all 6 Broken Places. And, with many of them, I have been surprised (though I shouldn't be) at how they developed a passion for their calling very early in life.

So . . . think back. Could that be true of you? Did you experience pain—deep pain—early on? Has that informed how you look at others today who struggle? Or did you watch someone, perhaps a loved one, endure a long, grueling life of pain? How did that shape you?

Maybe God is shaping your mission in life through experience along with your gifting. Maybe in a very dark period of your existence a flame was lit.

Is this why your heart burns within you on this topic of pain?

Well then. What are you waiting for?

CHAPTER 5

STEWARDS

"To be unconcerned about the physical creation is to be either desperately ignorant or irresponsibly callous."

—Christopher Wright, *The Mission of God*

I grew up outside of Pittsburgh, Pennsylvania. One clear memory of my childhood, albeit a dark one, is that of pollution. I remember walking out our front door to head to school and noticing a film of soot covering everything. I recall running my finger through it on our outside windowsill. I can still see in my mind the huge smokestack across the river billowing out dark clouds of smoke from the coal-fired energy plant. And I have memories of looking down upon the Allegheny River as we crossed one of its numerous bridges, being appalled by the oil sheens and flotillas of trash.

It was all just gross to me then, but it didn't feel immoral or wrong. Then the massive publicity campaigns and legislative actions of the early 1970s shined a light on the problem. Earth Day (1970), the Clean Water Act (1970), and the Clean Air Act (1972) all raised public concern and awareness of the plight of living organisms, the environment, and the planet. And they led to significant reform, even in the industrial river valleys of Pittsburgh.

What I find interesting and disturbing as I look back is how silent the church, my church, was about this issue. Not once do I recall any spiritual authority in my life—not my pastor, my venerable Sunday School teachers, or my parents—making a link for me between the care of creation and my faith. As a matter of fact, I experienced quite the opposite. I always had a sense that, somehow, environmentalists were to be perceived as looney, liberal, tree-hugging, non-Christian hippies. In my growing-up world there was no such thing as a "green Christian" or a Christian environmentalist. And care for the creation just wasn't a thing, even in my undergraduate Bible school education. Never mentioned. Not once.

Fast forward. My home town and the one in which I now live are largely clean and attractive. The soot is gone, the air breathable, the rivers are clean(ish), and to a large extent, we've conquered our littering problem in the US. But it is clear this planet is still in distress and in decay. I've seen it with my own eyes and felt it in my own lungs in places like Port Au Prince, Haiti, New Delhi, India, and Nairobi, Kenya.

Let's get right into what seems to be the biggest decay issue of our time—the issue that has so many people worked up, angry, frustrated, and at each other's throats: global warming. Climate change attributed largely to the increased levels of atmospheric carbon dioxide produced by the use of fossil fuels. And this due to mankind. If you are an evangelical, it's quite likely that for many reasons you have never heard the truth about global warming. So, here's a quick breakdown:

> In the 19th century, scientists discovered that certain gases in the air trap and slow down heat that would otherwise escape to space. Carbon dioxide is a major player; without any of it in the air, the Earth would be a frozen wasteland.

Hard evidence shows that the extra gas is coming from human activity. Carbon dioxide levels rose and fell naturally in the long-ago past, but those changes took thousands of years. Humans are now pumping the gas into the air much faster than nature has ever done.

Over the coming 25-30 years, we can expect to experience more extreme weather. Coral reefs and other sensitive habitats are already starting to die. If you don't see the connection, let me point you to places like Haiti where a massive hurricane has wiped out the infrastructure of an entire country. If that's not close enough to home, look at the devastation to New Orleans, which still has not fully recovered from Hurricane Katrina in 2005. And, there are huge segments of California destroyed by wildfires that resulted from severe drought, the impact of which remains to be seen.

Because of sea level rise, for instance, some 83,000 more residents of New York and New Jersey were flooded during Hurricane Sandy than would have been the case in a stable climate, scientists have calculated. Tens of thousands of people are already dying in heat waves made worse by global warming. The refugee flows that have destabilized politics around the world have been traced in part to climate change. Of course, as with almost all other social problems, poor people will be hit first and hardest.

The ocean has accelerated and is now rising at a rate of about a foot per century, forcing governments and property owners to spend tens of billions of dollars fighting coastal erosion. But even if that rate continued, it would probably be manageable, experts say. The risk is that the rate will increase still more. Many experts believe that even if emissions stopped tomorrow, 15-20 feet of sea level rise is already inevitable, enough to flood many cities unless trillions of dollars are spent protecting them. How long it will take is unclear. But if emissions continue at this pace, the ultimate rise could be 80-100 feet.[43]

You can guess by now how I feel about this issue. The very fact that one of the broken places of the world, in my opinion, is DECAY of the planet, will tell you where I stand. This is a pressing issue and should be a major priority, as concerning to us as the other five broken places.

In addition to global warming, here are just a few of the other ways this planet, this physical creation, is in stress and in decay:

- Pollution may not appear to be as big a problem in the US as it once was, but elsewhere it is creating crises. Estimates indicate that as many as 7 million people die premature deaths per year as a result.

- Our oceans are filled with items that do not belong there. Huge amounts of consumer plastics, metals, rubber, paper, textiles, derelict fishing gear, vessels, and other lost or discarded items enter the marine environment every day, making marine debris one of the most widespread pollution problems facing the world's oceans and waterways.

- The removal of a forest or stands of trees to convert the land to farms, ranches, or urban use led to the loss of nearly 1.6 million miles of forests around the world. Only 2.4 million square miles remain of the original 6 million square miles of forest that formerly covered the earth.

- Today, 1 in 9 people lack access to safe water.

- As many as 30 to 50 percent of all animal species are heading toward extinction in the next thirty years. Because every species' extinction potentially leads to the extinction of others bound to that species in this complex ecological web, numbers of extinctions are likely to snowball in the coming decades as ecosystems unravel.

"To abuse, pollute or destroy the natural order is to trample on the goodness of God in creation, to devalue what God values, to mute God's praise and to diminish God's glory."

—Christopher Wright, The Mission of God

If you find yourself tuning out as I list all of these statistics and signs of the decay of the planet, do me a favor and just take a look around you and imagine what this place, our home, was like when God created it. Stop and think for a moment about the natural resources he gave Adam and Eve and how our ancestors lived in harmony with the land, taking just what they needed and caring for it so it would continue to be there. Now consider what you see in the place of trees and streams and fertile fields. Is this what you imagine God intended us to have when he gave us this place to live? And then, think about how you would feel if you took the time and care to make a special gift for a loved one, knowing it would be just what they need to make their lives better, and they did nothing to care for it or, perhaps, they even used it as an ashtray or foot rest. Maybe these thoughts will be enough to get you concerned about this broken place.

What is A Steward?

A steward is one who responsibly manages something entrusted to their care. A steward manages the property of another. In the case of creation, the owner is God and His property is this planet. He made that abundantly clear.

> To the LORD your God belong the heavens,
> even the highest heavens, the earth and every-
> thing in it.
> —Deuteronomy 10:14

The creation is, by its very nature, a very good thing to God, not simply because human beings are in it. The earth has deep value to God whether we are around or not. It is not simply the box in which we play and live and exist. And, he fully expects we will care for it.

> Then God blessed them and said, "Be fruitful
> and multiply. Fill the earth and govern it. Reign
> over the fish in the sea, the birds in the sky, and
> all the animals that scurry along the ground."
> —Genesis 1:28

What did God mean when he said we should "govern" and "reign over" creation? Here's how my fellow pastor and friend, Tim Ayers, defines those words:

Some say that this was God giving us permission to do anything we wanted with the creation. They see this verse as the green light to aggressively take advantage of the creation for our own benefit. But the Hebrew words translated "govern" and "reign" mean, rather, someone stronger taking control of someone weaker in order to bring an ordering influence and to take charge for everyone's good. They mean to rule as someone's representative.

Simply, be a steward.

So, humanity must embrace our role as caretakers over the creation. We need to look out for it and see to its well-being. We do not have the right to use the creation to advance our perceived interests. Nor do we have the freedom to wantonly and ruthlessly abuse the creation. Creation needs to be cared for by someone strong, thoughtful, and wise. God wants that to be you.

And until we live up to that mandate, the planet, our world will wait in expectation.

> The creation waits in eager expectation for
> the sons of God to be revealed . . . in hope that
> the creation itself will be liberated from its
> bondage to decay and brought into the glorious
> freedom of the children of God.
>
> —Romans 8:18-21

Stewards: Healers of Creation

If your heart beats for this physical creation, undoubtedly your hero is Francis of Assisi, one of the most venerated religious figures in history. Francis founded a number of Roman Catholic orders that have had a significant impact on history, especially among the poor and suffering. But he is also remembered for his profound love of God's creation and the creatures therein.

It's tough to know if the stories of his interactions with creation are literally true or exaggerated, but they are, nonetheless, remarkable and inspiring.

There's the story of the birds. Francis and his companions were on a journey when, suddenly, Francis spotted a great number of birds of all varieties. Swept up in the moment, Francis left his friends in the road and ran after the birds. He greeted them in his usual way, expecting them to scurry off into the air as he spoke. But they didn't move. Filled with awe, he preached to them. "My brother and sister birds, you should praise your Creator and always love him: He gave you feathers for clothes, wings to fly and all other things that you need. It is God who made you noble among all creatures, making your home in thin, pure air. Without sowing or reaping, you receive God's guidance and protection." At this, the birds began to spread their wings, stretch their necks, and gaze at Francis, rejoicing and praising God in a wonderful way according to their nature. Francis then walked right through the middle of them, turned around and came back, touching their heads and bodies with his tunic.

Then there's the rabbit story. One day a brother brought a rabbit who had been caught in a trap to Francis. Francis advised the rabbit to be more alert in the future, then released the rabbit from the trap and set it on the ground to go its way. But the rabbit hopped back up onto Francis' lap, desiring to be close to him.

Apparently, even fish were also known to obey Francis. Whenever a fish was caught and Francis was nearby, he would return the fish to the water, warning it not to be caught again. On several occasions the fish would linger awhile near the boat, listening to Francis preach, until he gave them permission to leave. Then they would swim off.[44]

If you are driven to a destiny as a STEWARD of Gods' creation you *love* those stories, don't you? Or, if not Francis of Assisi , then John Muir the Scottish-born naturalist inspires you.

He has been called «The Father of our National Parks,» «Wilderness Prophet,» and «Citizen of the Universe.» He once described himself as a «poetico-trampo-geologist-botanist and ornithologist-naturalist." His influence on our nation and those of you who bleed for the planet is immeasurable. Muir, a passionate lover of God, also loved God's physical world.

"I only went out for a walk and finally concluded to stay out till sundown, for going out, I found, was really going in."

"This grand show is eternal. It is always sunrise somewhere; the dew is never dried all at once; a shower is forever falling; vapor is ever rising. Eternal sunrise, eternal dawn and gloaming, on sea and continents and islands, each in its turn, as the round earth rolls."

"The clearest way into the Universe is through a forest wilderness."

"Thousands of tired, nerve-shaken, over-civilized people are beginning to find out that going to the mountains is going home; that wildness is a necessity; and that mountain parks and reservations are useful not only as fountains of timber and irrigating rivers, but as fountains of life."[45]

If you are a STEWARD, a healer of DECAY in creation, those sentiments fire you up and empower you to be not just a STEWARD but an environmental activist. Patagonia founder and outdoor enthusiast Yvon Chouinard said, "If you think about all the gains our society has made, from independence to now, it wasn't government. It was activism. People think, 'Oh, Teddy Roosevelt established Yosemite National Park, what a great president.' B.S. It was John Muir who invited Roosevelt out and then convinced him to ditch his security and go camping. It was Muir, an activist, a single person."[46]

There is this perception of STEWARDS. There are nicknames. There are taunts. If this is your calling, then you've heard them: "hippie" or "tree hugger." But you're okay with that, because you decided long ago that it didn't matter what people thought of you. You can withstand the eye rolling and the push-back. You can handle the accusations of being a liberal. Bring it on. Because you care *that* much about the creation.

This broken place is not necessarily a physically dangerous one to engage in. Living *brave, not safe* likely won't mean you have to risk your health. But you will have to risk your reputation. Especially if you claim to be a follower of Jesus. It is not yet safe in some Christian circles to be vegan or take a stand about man-made greenhouse gasses. People don't get it. But that's okay, isn't it?

Keep on going, STEWARD of the planet and the

animals! You are a masterpiece of God created for such a time as this and for such works as these. There are lots of people just like you out there. And they want to meet you!

Here, are some more real stories of real STEWARDS who, perhaps like you, are trying desperately to bring healing to this world and its creatures and call others to action.

SARA STERLEY

If you asked most eight-year-old girls what they would like for their birthday, you'd expect them to say some kind of doll, a crafty thing, a stuffed animal, a game, or maybe some clothes. You wouldn't expect an eight-year-old to say she wanted a compost bin, yet that's exactly what Sara asked for on her eighth birthday. Sara Sterley had a strong sense of calling on her life from the get-go. She remembers at a very young age, seven or eight years old, advocating for her family to put filled 2-liter bottles in their toilet tank to conserve water. Where does a young kid come up with such an environmentally precocious attitude? "My parents weren't hippies. I just think God put this in my heart at a very young age," Sara says.

Her passion for creation care took a noticeable jump when her mom helped her find a book from the library called *50 Simple Things Kids Can Do to Save the Earth* by Earthworks Group. As she approached high school graduation she was even considering studying environmental law. That was not her destiny, but her environmental activism continued. As she puts it, "I did it covertly."

After Sara and her husband, Grant, joined Grace Church, she became known (in her words) as "the green person." She believed "Christians should be leading the way," and she made it her goal to "get people reconnected with creation." It occurred to her that in the suburban context, one way to get people's attention was through food, "the way to the suburban heart." So she took the lead in launching "Project Eden," whose mission is to reconnect people with the creation and to restore broken ecosystems.

A large component of Project Eden is the huge organic communal garden they created on the north end of our property. Sara sees gardening as "a revolutionary act" when done in a way that prioritizes care for the creation and healthy eating with a focus on "nutrient density." Under Sara's leadership, the Project Eden garden grew to a size that now provides a large percentage of the organic produce offered through Grace Church's choice food pantry. And they have branched out beyond the garden on Grace's property to restore our huge front pond to a wetland habitat. In addition, Project Eden (now hundreds of people strong), has made a pollinator prairie near the garden and even created a forest that supports native birds. Sara has led a green revolution! In some ways she is a prophet for healing this broken place.

She believes that creation is a "thin space"—a place where the boundary between Heaven and Earth is especially thin and God can be experienced more readily. She also is concerned that "decay of the planet is a justice issue in greater ways, as it has a disproportionate effect on the poor." Sara is totally aware of how she is perceived. "I own it; I'm a hippie tree-hugger!," and she is resolute in her commitment to do what she can to stimulate the body of Christ to join her in caring for his very good creation. Her passion goes way beyond avocation or personal preference. This is a calling. Sara says, "God needs me!"

NOAH GOLLAND

"I was fed up not knowing where I fit in." That was Noah Golland a few years ago. For years he had labored under the impression that he was to be a youth pastor. And, though he loves kids and still serves as a volunteer in student ministry, he came to realize that his calling lay elsewhere. But where, exactly? He found himself in what he called "a purposeless desert."

So Noah started praying and paying attention to his heart, what he enjoyed, what moved him. He came to a simple realization: he loved being outdoors, so much so that he and his wife, Leah, and their kids make it a regular habit to get outside and hike. It was while praying that he realized the broken place of DECAY bothered him greatly, and while hiking came to the conclusion "maybe we have a responsibility here."

His heart was stirred. And then God used circumstances to seal the deal.

As our church's Senior Director of Facilities, Noah realized he could help shape the entire organization's posture toward care of the creation. He is leading us in conducting a whole -church energy audit, and has been slowly reshaping our habits toward turning off lights, powering down computers, and eliminating plastic—simple stuff that has a huge impact. In addition, Noah is installing energy consumption software and is shifting us to LED lighting.

But the biggest game changer for Noah came recently when Project Eden came back under the auspices of Grace Church. He suddenly was given a large platform on which to live out his emerging calling. The huge communal organic garden and pond reclamation project and replanted native forest on our church's property are now under his stewardship. Noah will now have the privilege of leveraging these wonderful projects to create a new Creation Care Team at Grace and lead hundreds more people with his passion for the environment! They'll hear him say, "Get outside! We won't care until we get out in it!"

OLIVIA RODRIGUEZ

Olivia, my daughter-in-law, has a deep passion for creation care. Her deliberate decision to become a steward of it on behalf of God was born in a deeply traumatic moment. While on a mission trip with a youth group to East Africa she experienced for the first time and firsthand the slaughter of an animal, a goat, for everyone's evening meal. At seventeen years old, she didn't really understand yet why she was reacting so emotionally to something that everyone else seemed to be enjoying and celebrating. And when she was scolded for being so emotional, she turned inward and suppressed her passion through the rest of high school.

But, in time, her concern for animal welfare began to grow and she started to understand the depth of her emotions while watching documentaries like "Forks Over Knives." It all came to a head while on a trip with our family to the farm country of Pennsylvania. We all stayed together in a large B&B located in the middle of a working farm. Liv had never spent much time at all up close and personal with farm animals. Something clicked. It came together in her mind and heart, and a week later she began her vegetarian/vegan lifestyle, which she maintains to this day.

Liv said, "Once I made the connection to what's going on . . . that you are eating a life . . . I didn't want any part of that." She also is clear that this is no fad and she has made huge changes to her life to adapt.

In addition to the veganism, she is careful to, whenever possible, use cruelty-free products. She says, "It's not hard to find cruelty-free products . . . just Google it!" She is not unwilling to spend a bit more to ensure that no animals were harmed in the production of the thing she is consuming.

She and my son, Barry, have committed to purposely care for animals, providing a great life and space for animals to flourish. Olivia, as she can, also seeks to exert a gentle influence or advocacy for animals. Although she admits, "I'll never do it right or graciously. It's so hard to balance my low-grade fever of sadness with being gentle and gracious."

Perhaps the most surprising aspect of Liv's passion to be a steward of creation is the impact it has had on her life with God. She says, "This issue has kind of worked backward for me. Traditionally you would believe in God, figure out what that means for you, then find your passion for animals and God's creation. But I found this thing I'm passionate about and I've found God through it. This isn't a fad for me. I'm figuring out what God is into . . . and I think he's into this. This is who I understand God to be and what he cares about. I don't know how other people do the creation care thing without God in the equation. I would find it totally hopeless without him."

A side note...I suspect that some of you do not share Olivia's perspective on animal welfare. For that matter, you may not agree with me on my concern about global warming. Furthermore, as you work your way through the numerous stories I've told of people committed to healing this world on behalf of the Kingdom of God, you may not see eye-to-eye with a few of them. You may not share their theology or ideology. And that's fine. But don't miss the reason why their stories are told here. Don't miss their passion. Don't miss their intentionality. Don't miss their calling and their drive to discover their destiny. Compare their purposefulness with your own.

Dawna Markova in her excellent book *I Will Not Die an Unlived Life* says, "Living on purpose requires us to find what we love fiercely, give it all we've got, and then pass it on, as if it were a torch, to those who follow." That's what Olivia is trying to do. So are Heath, and Vic, and Chuck, and Sharon, and I pray to God, so am I.

What about you?

How to Step into Your Steward Calling

If you never thought of yourself as a STEWARD of creation, but you find your heart curiously stirred, then read on. The creation needs you, as it cannot advocate or fight for itself. The creation needs us to be the caregivers our Creator intended us to be. That is how the system God designed is supposed to work.

> "The creation needs us to be the caregivers our Creator intended us to be. That is how the system God designed is supposed to work."

Here are a few steps to healing creation on your own *Path of Yes.*

PARTNER WITH CREATION-CARE ORGANIZATIONS

There are a multitude of environmental organizations, secular and faith-based, whose mission is to protect the earth. The secular/governmental ones such as the EPA, Greenpeace, World Wildlife Fund (WWF), etc. get a lot of attention and are widely known. I want to point to a few faith-based groups, because Christians have not been leading the way in creation care and it is time for that to change.

There are a growing number of Christian creation-care organizations that would love to help you find your calling in healing the DECAY of our planet. Here's how they describe themselves:

Project Eden - Project Eden began in 2013 in Noblesville, Indiana with a mission to reconnect people with the creation and to restore broken ecosystems. We help people engage with, understand, appreciate, and steward the creation, thus enhancing their worship of God and the quality of their and others' lives. We view this as part of the process of helping people become faithful followers of Christ.

The Evangelical Environmental Network - The Evangelical Environmental Network (EEN) is a ministry that educates, inspires, and mobilizes Christians in their effort to care for God's creation, to be faithful stewards of God's provision, to get involved in regions of the United States and the world impacted by pollution, and to advocate for actions and policies that honor God and protect the environment.

Blessed Earth – Blessed Earth exists to inspire faithful stewardship of all creation. It is motivated by the Biblical mandate to care for God's creation. Blessed Earth promotes individual and group actions that encourage responsible stewardship of resources. It also builds bridges within and beyond the Church that serve the kingdom and glorify God.

PRAY FOR GOD'S CREATION

Here are a few prayers that might guide you as you intercede to the Lord of the cosmos on behalf of our planet.

*O God, enlarge within us the sense of
fellowship with all living things,
our brothers the animals to whom thou
gavest the earth as their home in
common with us.
We remember with shame that in the past
we have exercised the high dominion
of man with ruthless cruelty
so that the voice of the earth,
which should have gone up to thee
in song, has been a groan of travail.
May we realize that they live not for
us alone but for themselves and for
thee, and that they love
the sweetness of life.*
—St. Basil the Great[47]

Lord, help us to maintain a reverent attitude towards nature, threatened from all sides today, in such a way that we may restore it completely to its role of usefulness to all humankind for the glory of God the Creator.
— Franciscan prayer[48]

*O God,
We thank you for this earth, our home; for the wide sky
and the blessed sun, for the ocean and streams, for the
towering hills and the whispering wind, for the trees
and green grass.
We thank you for our senses by which we hear the songs
of birds, and see the splendor of fields of golden wheat,
and taste autumn's fruit, rejoice in the feel of snow, and*

smell the breath of spring flowers.
Grant us a heart opened wide to all this beauty; and
save us from being so blind that we pass unseeing when
even the common thornbush is aflame with your glory.
For each new dawn is filled with infinite possibilities for
new beginnings and new discoveries. Life is constantly
changing and renewing itself. In this new day of new
beginnings with God, all things are possible. We are re-
stored and renewed in a joyous awakening to the won-
der that our lives are and, yet, can be.

—unknown[49]

Creator God,
you formed us from the dust of the earth,
and reveal your fingerprints in all flesh.
Teach us your deep wisdom
in the order and beauty of all that you have made.
When our care for your creation is found wanting,
reprove and reform us,
so that our footprints may be more gentle on the earth,
tending and keeping it as your own handiwork,
through Jesus Christ our Lord. Amen.

—Anglican Church of Australia[50]

This particular broken place would lend itself well to keeping a prayer journal or scrapbook to help guide your intercession. Or find kindred spirits who are called to heal DECAY and form a prayer team around it.

MAKE PERSONAL LIFESTYLE ADJUSTMENTS
We have an individual responsibility to care for the creation and step into the role of STEWARD, whether it is a calling or not, and it is our duty as part of God's creation. To do that, you

may have to make some changes to the way you live. Most of these ideas come from Sara Sterley who I featured above.

1. Pay attention to how much you consume and what you consume:
   o how much you eat and what you eat
   o the energy consumed by your vehicles and machinery
   o the energy and water consumption of your household

Sara: "We practice 'no screen night' on Sundays and Mondays. We read books or play games, which is not only a reset for each of us, but it means that we're not pummeled by advertising, fueling materialism and consumerism. Also, screens use electricity. Instead, we're sitting around a lamp reading a book or playing a game."

2. Pay attention to how you buy, not just how much but from whom. Which of the companies that you purchase from have ethically sound environmental policies?

Sara: "We try to buy local. I think we should all be buying far less in general, but this is one that I think you could really get suburbanites on board with. Christians shouldn't just worry about how they give their money; they should think strategically about how they spend it, and that could really change the world by seemingly small actions. Buy local food from local farmers, support local restaurants (and maybe just pick a few to really throw your support behind and build relationships there), seek out sustainably-produced products. We create the types of communities we want to live in by how we spend our dollars. If we spend our grocery dollars at the farmer's markets (and new options like Market Wagon) instead of big box grocers, we're sending a loud message to farmers and business owners of the type of community we want."

3. Pay attention to how you dispose of things. Recycle and reuse.
4. Limit disposable packaging and use cloth napkins.
5. Practice mindfulness in your eating and food preparation:
   o stay at home, cook at home, slow down
   o consider the benefits of a plant-based diet to reduce global warming, increase your health and practice animal compassion
   o eat seasonally

Sara: " We have learned so much about ourselves and God by being more thoughtful in this way. So much of the Bible has to do with an agricultural society/calendar, so living by that ourselves opens up so much more about the character of God and God's people throughout history. It also connects us more intimately with creation by virtue of living more in line with the seasons."

6. Use a bike as much as possible.

Sara: "Like eating seasonally, bike riding is harder, more time-consuming, and sweatier than the alternative of jumping in the car; but, it is also infinitely more rewarding for our physical health, obviously, but also our mental health and the family time in creation that it affords."

7. Limit air travel.

Sara: "We love to travel, but we prefer to go somewhere that we can drive to because it uses far less fossil fuels. Or just stay home."

PARTNER WITH YOUR LOCAL CHURCH

We are nowhere near where we should be as a congregation in being mindful of our impact on the physical creation, but here are a few things our church has done to upgrade our environmental sensitivity:

- We recycle.

- We had an energy management system installed for about ¾ of the building to better regulate heating/AC.

- We installed sensors for the bathroom lights so they don't get left on all day.

- We designed our whole building and its rooms as multi-use for generations to come.

- We used precast concrete panels as a sustainable method for building enclosure with internal building insulation. They also were locally manufactured with less transportation carbon footprint.

- At our newest campus property, instead of a large retention pond that would have led to the destruction of many trees, we created a number of smaller areas to absorb, collect, and slow down storm water runoff. This left untouched a large section of trees and grassy areas. Throughout the project, plant species were chosen to reduce maintenance and irrigation needs, provide habitat for wildlife, and restore degraded areas of the site that had succumbed to erosion problems.

LEAD YOUR COMPANY OR BUSINESS

There are thousands of companies that are leading the way in environmental sustainability. Here are a few whose goals and dreams I found fascinating:

Unilever – (Hellman's Mayo, Lipton Tea, Ben and Jerry's, Axe deodorant) They describe their efforts in creation care this way: "The Unilever Sustainable Living Plan (USLP) is our blueprint for achieving our vision to grow our business, whilst decoupling our environmental footprint from our growth and increasing our positive social impact. The Plan sets stretching targets, including how we source raw materials and how consumers use our brands. By 2030 our goal is to halve the environmental footprint of the making and use of our products as we grow our business."

Specifically, they want to cut the greenhouse gas impact of their products across the lifecycle, the water associated with the consumer use of their products, and the waste associated with the disposal of their products in half by 2030. And finally, by 2020 they want to source 100% of their agriculture raw materials sustainably.[51]

Waste Management (who removes my trash every Tuesday morning) says clearly that, "At Waste Management, we care about the planet. We feel a responsibility to leave it to future generations in better shape than we were given it."

Most interesting to me is their Think Green® initiative. "When we Think Green, we think of a world...where there are so many clean, alternative ways to produce power that the threat of exhausting our natural resources is forever put to rest."[52]

Of course you would expect **Patagonia**, makers of high-end outdoor apparel, to have an eye toward environmental sensitivity. "The quality of Patagonia depends, to a large degree, on whether we can reduce our impact on the environment. This means auditing the materials and methods we use to make our products, taking responsibility for the entire lifecycle of our products and examining how we use resources at our buildings and facilities."

But, what got my attention wasn't their commitment to alternative natural fibers and recycled materials, but their creation of Worn Wear—an online store where you can purchase used Patagonia clothing. And you can trade in your old gear as well. Here's how they describe it. "One of the most responsible things we can do as a company is to make high-quality stuff that lasts for years and can be repaired, so you don't have to buy more of it. Worn Wear celebrates the stories we wear, keeps your gear in action longer through repair and reuse, and recycles your garments when they're beyond repair."[53]

Now, what can *you* do to influence your business to join the efforts of others to heal the decay of our world?

BECOME A PUBLIC ADVOCATE
Perhaps your gifts of communication coupled with a clear passion for God's creation can be leveraged to have a profound

effect on others. Tim Ayers, himself a man committed to this good creation, once said in a sermon:

> My hope is that we will be people that stand up as leaders in the fight against any destruction of the environment that comes from mankind's misdirected priorities, wherever it occurs. My hope is that Christians would be on the forefront of speaking out about all kinds of quality of life issues related to the creation. Things like zoning, public parks, mass transit, pedestrian accessibility to services, and water quality control. These all have a direct impact on people's lives and they have a direct impact on the environment.[54]

You, Again

What are you thinking right now? People who have a passion for the environment need little motivation. People committed to healing DECAY, largely, are getting after it. But what about those of you who have never felt the freedom to express your concern about God's creation? Concerned about being politically incorrect in your sphere of influence?

Well, what about this: maybe God created you as his masterpiece specifically to bring healing to the decay that breaks his heart. So, let me nudge you. It's okay. You have all the endorsement of Heaven to get your hands dirty in the battle to restore the goodness of creation.

Go on. Get a composter. Stop eating meat if you feel led. Start a blog. Rally your family or your church or your community . . .

. . . and save the planet and animals and water and the atmosphere. We'll follow your lead.

CHAPTER 6
ACTIVISTS

"When it comes to racism, there is only one side: to stand against it."
—Cardinal Blase Cupich,
the Archdiocese of Chicago

On August 12, 2017, America blew up. All the simmering racial tension and animosity within the United States suddenly boiled over in Emancipation Park, Charlottesville, Virginia. White supremacists, neo-Nazis, and neo-Confederates gathered there to oppose the removal of a statue of Robert E. Lee. Some came armed with Confederate battle flags, some with anti-Semitic banners, and others with semi-automatic rifles. It was a loud, raucous, fury-filled protest. When counter-protestors confronted the marchers it turned violent, leaving fourteen injured. Later that day, a man linked to a white supremacist group rammed his car into a group of counter-protestors injuring nineteen and killing one. It was as if someone knocked the lid off a boiling caldron of hate and tipped it over.

But this pot has been simmering and bubbling for as long as I can remember. Racial suspicion, prejudice, fear, and ethnic slurring swirled around my community in my growing-up years. I'd like to say nothing has changed in the past sixty years . . . but, that's not true. It's gotten way worse.

We were primed for Charlottesville by a series of tragic events, political movements, and cultural shifts that have sparked enormous waves of frustration and even more hate:

- a sustained series of attacks since the 1970s by Islamic terrorists that have killed tens of thousands of innocent people;

- the mass influx of immigrants into the West from the war-torn Middle East, from the economically struggling and violence-ridden African continent, and from Latin America;

- the rise of nationalism in the West that has spawned major political shifts and the development of ultra-nationalist hate groups;

- the killings of black men, some at the hands of law enforcement, inflaming fury—Trayvon Martin, Michael Brown, Tamir Rice, Philando Castile, names we won't soon forget;

- racially motivated mass murders in a Charleston church and apparent retaliatory mass killings of cops in Dallas and Baton Rouge;

- the rise of hate crimes in general, two years in a row for the first time in a decade, according to a recent FBI report, amassing to roughly 250,000 hate crimes per year in America;

- the upsurge in protest movements as a reaction to much of what has already been listed— the hate and debate finding its way beyond the news media into churches and even professional sports.

It was only a matter of time until a Charlottesville would happen. And it is only a matter of time until it happens somewhere, somehow, again. What a terribly broken place is HATRED!

And, of course, nothing is new under the sun. Long before the events of today were the hellish, evil-inspired, hate-filled genocides of the past. Dozens of them: the Holocaust of the 1940s, Cambodia in the late 1970s, Rwanda of 1994, just to name a few—all of them fueled by the same tragic mix of bigotry, racism, nationalism, and dehumanization.

I guess you could say that hatred is humanity's third sin—the first being the disobedience of Adam and Eve and the second their own son Cain's murder of his brother Abel. We have been hating, murdering, and destroying human lives ever since.

This broken place begins in the mind or heart, or more accurately, the gut. Hatred starts with us-versus-them. *They are different from me, I prefer to be with people like me, and I am suspicious of people who are not like me.* This leads to segregation, ethnocentricity, racial seclusion, and discrimination. In time, hatred breeds bigotry and intolerance. *You are not like me and I don't like you.* Ultimately, hatred becomes dehumanization. *I hate you so very much that I see you as less than human.* And when we begin to perceive others as less than human, well, it becomes easy to enslave, attack, harm, and kill.

It's tough to assign one word to describe this hellish system, but *hate* comes closest. It begins with an attitude followed by an insult and epithet, and it ends with a gun or barrel bomb or suicide vest.

Hatred kills. But it also plays out in religious radicalization, ideological extremism, and political fanaticism. It shows up in ugly road rage, cable news zealotry, generational misogyny, corporate maliciousness, and even church business meetings (I've been there). But here, early in the twenty-first century, hatred most often expresses itself in America's original and prevailing sin: racism.

It was in 1619 that Dutch pirates seized a Spanish slave ship. In so doing, they captured nineteen African slaves from the Spanish. They took them to Jamestown, Virginia, where they were promptly sold. In that moment, slavery was born in America. What followed, to date, has been the most horrifying, hate-filled 250 years in our nation's history—12.5 million slaves were shipped to America, nearly two million died in route, countless millions died thereafter, and racism became the ugly underbelly of America.

Hatred has ruled our American psyche for 400 years, and racism is the recurring cancer that bedevils us daily. Despite the desperate civil rights movement of the 1950s and 60s, racism (hatred) remains virtually untouched.

Just recently, in the wake of all the unrest following the police shootings of young black men and the resurgence of white supremacists after the 2016 election, the largest evangelical denomination in America felt it necessary to draft this resolution at its most recent convention:

WHEREAS, Racism and white supremacy are, sadly, not extinct but present all over the world in various white supremacist movements, sometimes known as "white nationalism" or "alt-right"; now, therefore, be it RESOLVED, That the messengers to the Southern Baptist Convention, meeting in Phoenix, Arizona, June 13–14, 2017, decry every form of racism, including alt-right white supremacy, as antithetical to the Gospel of Jesus Christ; and be it further RESOLVED, That we denounce and repudiate white supremacy and every form of racial and ethnic hatred as of the devil; and be it further RESOLVED, That we acknowledge that we still must make progress in rooting out any remaining forms of intentional or unintentional racism in our midst; and be it further RESOLVED, That we earnestly pray, both for those who advocate racist ideologies and those who are thereby deceived, that they may see their error through the light of the Gospel, repent of these hatreds, and come to know the peace and love of Christ through redeemed fellowship in the Kingdom of God, which is established from every nation, tribe, people, and language.[55]

It passed. But only after days of rancor, backlash, and controversy . . . among its pastors.

Don't miss that . . . *its pastors.*

Over dinner not long ago, a black pastor friend of mine said, "We're sitting on a powder keg. This is a watershed moment." I have to agree.

Mi nombre es David Diego Rodriguez ¡pero no hablo Espanol! Translation: My name is David Diego Rodriguez, but I don't speak Spanish! (Well, that's about the limit of the Spanish I speak.) I am one quarter Spanish, but the rest of me is decidedly *gringo*. I am a peachy Caucasian. My grandfather emigrated to the US from Spain early in the twentieth century and died when I was three. (Ironically, he entered the US illegally through Canada).

But, that name of mine, despite my pale presentation, has caused me some amount of issues—mostly innocuous, like when our drunk neighbor called me a Mexican bastard, or when a past potential employer said in a phone interview, "You're not Irish, are you?" Ha.

But in the last five years I've had a more serious issue to deal with. Nearly every time I've re-entered the US from international travel, I've been detained for secondary screening. I've asked border agents why. Most ignore me, but a couple have suggested that, indeed, it is because of my name. I went so far as to be interviewed and approved for the Global Entry program to get expedited clearance. Didn't work. Still detained.

The most recent time was in Chicago where I was escorted to a separate room for secondary screening. After about fifteen minutes, an agent walked into the room with my passport and yelled, "David Rodriguez! ¿donde?" I don't speak Spanish, but I knew he had yelled, "Where are you?," and, believe me, he did it with what felt like great condescension. I felt it. He thrust my passport back at me and dismissed me, physically and emotionally. This was a very minor inconvenience—nothing in the bigger scope of things—but, in that moment, I experienced a hint of the feeling other people have to deal with on a daily basis.

One more personal reflection: One of the great joys of Penny's and my life is the family we unofficially adopted a number of years ago. Chris and Victoria, along with their kids, Isabella, Anya, and Jude, are as much family to us as our two biological kids and their spouses. The three kids call us Nana and Papa. We love them dearly. As we have journeyed together, and the children have gotten older, we've had to face the near certain reality of racial profiling, for they are biracial. Chris, their dad, an African-American man, certainly has dealt with it, as has Victoria, who is of Mexican lineage. We realize the kind of world these kids, especially Jude, are growing into. I know Jude and his dad will someday have "the talk" about being a black man in America. Jude is so sweet and tender and just lights up a room when he enters. The thought of having to prepare him for being profiled just breaks my heart. Knowing he will be hated and will arouse suspicion just because of the color of his skin makes me furious.

So, yeah, this is personal.

Not only is ethnic hatred and racism breeding violence and fury, but it is perpetuating a system in which the gap in fairness of treatment, access to education, and achievement for minorities continues to widen.

- The public school suspension rate among US black and Native American students is almost three times that for whites.

- Black, Latino, and Native American children are more than twice as likely as white children to drop out of school.

- As of 2010, white families, on average, earned about $2 for every $1 that black and Hispanic families earned.

- A black boy born in America has a 1 in 3 chance of going to prison in his lifetime and a Latino boy has a 1 in 6 chance; a white boy—1 in 17.

- A report by the Department of Justice found that blacks and Hispanics were approximately three times more likely to be searched during a traffic stop than white motorists.

Hatred and racism not only kill and perpetuate injustice, but they also cause deep and lasting pain.

The emotional and relational toll of hatred and racism is inestimable. In a recent *New York Times* article, Ekow Yankahnov reflected on how he must help his son process the inevitable racism he will encounter:

> It is impossible to convey the mixture of heartbreak and fear I feel for [my son]. [The 2016] election has made it clear that I will teach my boys the lesson generations old, one that I for the most part nearly escaped. I will teach them to be cautious, I will teach them suspicion, and I will teach them distrust. Much sooner than I thought I would, I will have to discuss with my boys whether they can truly be friends with white people.

> History has provided little reason for people of color to trust white people in this way, and these recent months have put in the starkest relief the contempt with which the country measures the value of racial minorities.

> As against our gauzy national hopes, I will teach my boys to have profound doubts that friendship with white people is possible. When they ask, I will teach my sons that their beautiful hue is a fault line. Spare me platitudes of how we are all the same on the inside. I first have to keep

my boys safe, and so I will teach them before the world shows them this particular brand of rending, violent, often fatal betrayal.

Imagining we can now be friends across this political line is asking us to ignore our safety and that of our children, to abandon personal regard and self-worth.[56]

Wow. That is just so very hard to process. What a terribly broken place this is! So very broken.

Our forefathers wrote into our Declaration of Independence:

"We hold these truths to be self-evident, that all men are created equal, that they are endowed by their Creator with certain unalienable Rights, that among these are Life, Liberty and the pursuit of Happiness."

This was the foremost of the "causes" set forth by our nation's founders to articulate why they were declaring independence from England. In that document, they indicated these "truths" came directly from the Laws of Nature and Nature's God. I believe they had as their inspiration these words of Scripture: "God created human beings in his own image. In the image of God he created them; male and female he created them." (Genesis 1:27)

Every single human being, regardless of ethnicity, nationality, or race, carries in themselves the very image of the God who created them. The meaning of that truth has been studied and debated ever since Moses first wrote it and passed it along to the people of God who had just crossed the dry ground of the Red Sea. No matter how you exegete that passage some things are indeed "self-evident." All humans are unequivocally equal. Every human being bears the right to live. No human being, inherently, should have to endure withering hatred. These are just a few of the implications that come to bear on God's view of this particular broken place.

I recently read a fascinating article in the online magazine *Faithfully*. Erna Kim Hackett, Associate National Director for Urban Programs with InterVarsity Christian Fellowship/USA, writes of her strong conviction that we must shift from discussing racial reconciliation to confronting white supremacy.

She suggests, "We are working within a profoundly broken theological framework." Her observations: "Watching white Christians and people of color submitted to whiteness respond again and again with denial of systemic injustice; disregard for the lived experience of black people; silence in the pulpit; a deeply ingrained superiority regarding issues of race; and a fixation on intentions over outcomes, I had to ask why those discipled by the racial reconciliation framework were so ill-equipped to engage, learn from and respond to a movement focused on systemic and institutionalized racial injustice."

She continued:

"White theology, in profound syncretism with American culture, has distorted the Bible to be solely about individual redemption. So it is blind to the reality that when Scripture says, 'I know the plans I have for you,' the *you* is plural and addressed to an entire community of people that has been displaced and is in exile. All Scripture has been reduced to individual interactions between God and a person, even when the interactions are actually between God and a community, or Jesus and a group of people. As a result, white theology defines racism as hateful thoughts and deeds by an individual, but cannot comprehend communal, systemic or institutionalized sin because it has erased all examples of that framework from Scripture."[57]

Could it be that God takes this broken place of HATRED more personally than any of the others?

Here it is, the theological bottom line for the condemnation of hatred, racism, dehumanization, discrimination, ethnic supremacy, and of course, genocide: Every. Single. Human. Being. Made in the image of God. Absolute equality on a cosmic, divine scale.

Yet, as epic a truth as it is, it did not take humanity long to disregard it. By Genesis 11, "people spread out to various lands, each identified by its own language, clan, and national identity." (Genesis 10:5)

Races were born and tribalism became a thing. And we know where *that* led.

What Is an Activist?

Clearly, when Jesus began to lay out God's kingdom values, he did so deliberately upending centuries-held feelings about racism, nationalism, and prejudice. He embraced Samaritans, engaged Greeks, made heroes out of perceived pagans, and was open to dialogue with the hated Romans. His value system was clear:

- Love your enemies and pray for those who persecute you. (Matthew 5:44)

- Do to others what you would have them do to you. (Matthew 7:12)

- Blessed are the peacemakers, for they will be called sons of God. (Matthew 5:9)

He was an activist. He was a disruptor. He took on the institutions—the establishment, the power structures—intending to disrupt the rigid systems that had created division and fostered hatred. He sought to change that, to combat hatred with love.

And those who followed after him—His young disciples and early church leaders—took it upon themselves to become prophets of the inbreaking kingdom of open arms to all:

- In the body of Christ "there is no Greek or Jew, circumcised or uncircumcised, barbarian, Scythian, slave or free, but Christ is all, and is in all." (Colossians 3:11)

- "He tore down the wall we used to keep each other at a distance . . . Instead of continuing with two groups of people separated by centuries of animosity and suspicion, he created a new kind of human being, a fresh start for everybody." (Ephesians 2:13-14)

- "This is how we know we are in him. Anyone who claims to be in the light but hates his brother is still in the darkness." (1 John 2:9)

But my favorite image of love, reconciliation, and inclusiveness—one that I reflect on again and again and have preached on many times—comes from that odd book of the Revelation. Captured in all its weird and captivating imagery, this divine and supernatural daydream given to a man named John includes this powerful metaphor of what could be. John "sees" a city that I believe represents the personification of the fully realized Kingdom of God. And then he recalls:

> I saw no temple in the city, for the Lord God Almighty and the Lamb are its temple. And the city has no need of sun or moon, for the glory of God illuminates the city, and the Lamb is its light. The nations will walk in its light, and the kings of the world will enter the city in all their glory. Its gates will never be closed at the end of day because there is no night there. And all the nations will bring their glory and honor into the city.
>
> —Revelation 21:22-26

All the nations enter with "their honor and glory." To me, it pictures all their beautiful skin tones and languages and cultures coming together, bathed in the light of Jesus and the wonder of the Kingdom of God. God has never been color blind! He absolutely adores every variation of nationality and race, all created powerfully in his own image!

"God has never been color blind! He absolutely adores every variation of nationality and race, all created powerfully in his own image!"

And his never-ending quest is that we would join him in his activism and take up his cause to that end! But, it won't be easy. We've talked about the stigmas attached to the broken Places that make it difficult for healers to reach those in need. The healing role of activism itself carries stigma because activists are often presumed to be radical and break the law. When you start to work against entrenched hatred you are going to face a lot of challenges, because it won't just be a matter of rolling up your sleeves and fixing a broken system; it's a matter of changing hearts and minds, and that takes a special dedication. But don't let the stigma associated with being an activist dissuade you from standing up, speaking out, and fighting against whatever hatred you feel called to heal. I am so very glad that some of God's people have stepped into their calling to be ACTIVISTS against HATRED.

Activists: Healers of Hatred

With HATRED being a systemic/entrenched problem, those who are called to heal this broken place must be activists because it requires dedication, courage, and persistence to break structures that support hatred and division. It takes an unwavering commitment to the slow and steady re-shaping of the way people think and behave. It's not an easy task! As Jed Bartlet from the television show "West Wing" once said, "Change comes in excruciating increments for those who want it."

Any list of ACTIVISTS who have dedicated themselves to the broken place of HATRED would include names like Martin Luther King Jr., Rosa Parks, Frederick Douglass, William Wilberforce, and Mahatma Gandhi. However, likely not making any such lists would be Nick Chiles, an African American newspaper editor living in early 1900s in Topeka, Kansas.

Chiles was a "persistent provocateur." The consistent theme in Chiles's lifelong anti-racism activism: appeals to the Christian principles of white Americans. Chiles came to believe, as he explained in 1905, that his newspaper was not directed solely at the black community but was also a means of "educating the white man in the moral duty that he owes the colored man as a citizen of the United States of America."

He wrote this to a U.S. Senator who was an avowed white supremacist. "It is your Christian duty to help undo the great injustice that has been perpetrated upon them (black people). If this is accomplished you will merit the prayers of thousands, for there are many praying Christians of both races who are striving to bring about this change." Chiles firmly believed that the problem of racism in the United States was a spiritual problem that would not be solved until the consciences of white Christians could be awakened.

Nick Chiles eventually determined to try the impossible: to run for President of the United States. The year was 1926. To say this was quixotic is an understatement. His campaign platform included eight planks, most of them focused on ending Southern segregationist control of the Senate, re-enfranchising African Americans, and guaranteeing workers a living wage. It also included a plank that made Chiles's righteous indignation clear: "The Holy Bible for my Guide."[58]

Nick Chiles personifies what it takes to live as an ACTIVIST seeking healing in the broken place of HATRED. It takes courage beyond measure. It takes persistence over the long haul. It takes an unwavering commitment to the truth, especially as revealed in God's Word. But it also takes a willingness to be a firebrand, a meddler and agitator.

If this is your peculiar calling, this doesn't faze you, does it? Nope. You just shrug your shoulders, pick up your sign and march on like these folks.

MARC WILLIAMS

He's a renaissance man, hip hop artist, musician (working on his 10th recording project), DJ (aka Mr. Kinetic), but mostly a highly valued special education high school teacher. He calls himself "a black nerd." Whether he indeed is a nerd or not, he certainly is a gifted artist and considered cool by his students. Marc is also a social activist making extensive use of social media to provoke conversation and awareness. He seems to be more aware than most of the injustices of the day and is not shy about offering his perspective and concern. Of particular interest to him are issues of hatred and racism. It is not uncommon for Marc to have Twitter "conversations" and debates with anyone who'll engage with him, including some of the politicians he confronts with his social media posts.

And Marc is deliberate about it. Marc says, "I use my platform to speak truth. I work with and spend cultural currency. I've always felt comfortable with having something to say."

He comes by his boldness naturally. His dad, a military man, taught him early on to be an intellectual with a social activism mindset. "My dad taught me to live with a careful nosiness; to think through it and be ready with a response." Like most young African-American kids, Marc experienced the hatred of racism at an early age. He describes his middle school years as "tense though not outwardly hostile. Things were certainly not racially harmonious. It was, 'We're all over here and you're all over there'." He describes the first time he remembers being called the N-word: "My first instinct was to fight him." Instead, Marc began to build his cultural currency through his musical skills. "Music became a way of connecting with everyone. Music allowed me to be open to other cultures."

Marc came face to face with hatred at an unimaginable level on a mission trip with a team from our church. He joined a team travelling to Rwanda to engage with African Leadership and Reconciliation Ministries (ALARM) to understand the horrific effects of the genocide of 1994. He remembers it being "the most tangible, terrible example I've ever seen of racism blended with the lack of democracy." He was troubled deeply by the "bogus tribal stuff and the manufactured (ethnic) separation" he learned of. It fueled his passion to engage as many people as he can to "participate and pay attention" to the issues of injustice, hatred, and racism.

Marc is committed to being "abnormal and out of place" if necessary to generate conversation and expose truth. To Marc, that was the way of Jesus, his model. As a man of faith in Christ, Marc says he always imagines Jesus' words "in colloquial. He was plain-spoken and a model of associating with all." Sounds like Marc!

You'll find Marc these days on Twitter @MrKinetik (The Funky Educator) speaking, conversing, provoking thought, and healing. Marc: the hip hop prophet?

BRANDON CASHBURN

Brandon is not what you might label a typical activist dealing with racism. He's a midwestern white guy whose life experience, education, and early career have been just that: Midwestern white. Yes, he's had a few experiences dealing with racial issues in his work. And he did have one black accountability partner and friend in college, but outside of that his was a monochromatic world.

However, his world changed dramatically one day. Though not much of a documentary watcher previously, he responded to a colleague's challenge to see the movie *The*

13th. The film is titled after the Thirteenth Amendment to the United States Constitution that freed slaves and prohibited slavery in the United States. It explores the "intersection of race, justice, and mass incarceration" in our country.

The 13th rocked Brandon and caused him to think deeply about what he felt and believed about racism and hatred.

Then one day, while working out at the YMCA, he glanced up at a TV monitor to see the breaking news of the racial confrontation in Charlottesville. He sat a long time in the locker room processing, and then walked out of the Y bawling, thinking, *I've got to DO something!*

Brandon started reading everything he could get his hands on covering the subject. He did YouTube searches, listened to podcasts, and watched more documentaries. He told me, "My heart is pulling me and I'm being thrown down a path, but I feel like a baby in this." He has begun wondering whether his activism might lead him into political reform.

But in the meantime, he's been doing what he can. He has started the black students' association in his suburban high school where he's a teacher. And, along with a few other passionate activists from our church, he formed a conversation-generating group called "The Listening Table" which meets to be informed and speak about racism. I've been there. It's a way cool diverse group of folks unafraid to have honest conversations about this broken place.

Brandon may feel like a baby in this, but he's learning how to walk into this world of healing rather quickly!

JOANNA BURRESS

Joanna remembers vividly what it felt like to be "the other," the outsider, the one who was not like the others. Joanna felt the sting of discrimination.

As a little third grader in Hawaii it was clear she was one of only a very few white kids. The majority of her classmates were Asian-Pacific Islanders. Joanna says, "I stuck out like a sore thumb." For one, she was much taller than the other kids and even her teachers! And, she was ethnically monochromatic. She told me, "All the other kids could rattle off what percentage Hawaiian and like four other ethnicities that they were. And, I'm like, my last name is French. That's all I knew because I was coming from this majority culture where it didn't matter. I was just white."

She still recalls the discomfort of not knowing what family heritage food to bring on International Food day and the embarrassment of being given a hard time by a teacher when she tried to learn hula. She knew the teacher thought she had no business trying to learn that dance.

Perhaps most distressing to Joanna was being a white girl in a culture that she perceived felt ill will toward whites. "The word used for white people in Hawaii is *haole*, which literally means stranger and is used somewhat derogatorily but pretty commonly. And so, that was my experience with feeling like an outsider."

Maybe that early experience was what formed the foundation of the life she lives now. Joanna, thirty-four, a business analyst in a software company, living a thoroughly suburban life with her husband and three little boys, has become an activist using her skills and following her passion to bring healing to the broken place of HATRED, in particular, systemic racism.

Her first foray into an activist lifestyle came while she was a student at a Midwestern Christian college. Joanna says,"There I started to feel a kind of suffocation. Everybody not only looked alike but thought alike. I saw how people that lived in a bubble could not converse with the outside world." She said it felt as if her fellow students didn't care to consider the lives of people from other religions and races. So, in frustration she began writing letters to the editor of the school newspaper calling out the school and community for turning a blind eye to the needs of others in the world beyond campus and ignoring the history of racism in that very part of the country.

Post college, she and her husband bought a home in the suburbs and Joanna, a "news junkie," began to pay careful attention to the injustice, hatred and racism in our world. "I saw what happened to Trayvon Martin. That was one of the things that really started me seeing systemic racism." And the shooting of Tamir Rice devastated her. "What if it was my son that was playing in the park?"

In time, Joanna discovered at our church a group of like-minded activists trying to make sense of all the racism swirling around us and wondering if the church had the guts and will to address it. She faced a decision. "I'm either going to throw my hands up and leave the church, or I'm going to change it—change where I am."

She chose to be a part of the change. She threw herself into the work of the Listening Table—essentially, an ongoing conversation. People from all kinds of backgrounds, races, and ethnicities listening to one another and other activists, probing for solutions to the devastation of hatred.

Joanna serves as the "voice" of the Listening Table primarily through the group's social media outlets. Her goal is simple: "I'm trying to bring awareness. I feel like white evangelicals don't acknowledge that systematic racism is a problem. Knee-jerk white fragility doesn't let people look at themselves and admit that they themselves are part of the problem or part of the systems that are the problem. I'd love to even go beyond confessing that there is a problem to repenting of it corporately. We can't go to reconciliation until we've been through all that and worked on our own hearts. "

Joanna says that this conversation at the Listening Table is "under the radar now." With her passion and her mind and her skills, I don't think it will be for long.

How to Step into Your Activist Calling

Live brave, not safe.

Each broken place requires that commitment. But this one, HATRED, maybe more than any of the others. It is a brave thing to take a deep dive into your own soul. You must start there. You must root out any bad theology or latent prejudices or sense of racial supremacy if you plan to bring healing to HATRED. That takes real courage. That takes real work, confession, and repentance. It's too easy to resort to stereotypes and profiling when we look at someone who is "other" than us.

But it also takes a unique measure of bravery to wade into a world of racial posturing and political maneuvering around this topic. The language is vitriolic. The social media engagement is vicious. The accusations and finger pointing are venomous.

And do not forget how much of this broken place of HATRED is literally bristling with guns. Courage needed, indeed.

Take a step. Start with you, your heart. Do a deep dive and discover what you must face. Then with "palms-up" humility and listening ears start down the *Path of Yes*. The term ACTIVIST is not necessarily a positive one in all circles, is it? Some people sneer when they say it. But, for you . . . you kind of like it, don't you? It might even be your badge of courage!

DO YOUR THEOLOGICAL HOMEWORK

At the core of hatred is an ethnocentricity and tribalism that is at utter odds with the heart of God and his desire for community within the human race. So you, personally, must come to grips with God's theology of reconciliation. You need to get this settled in your mind and heart. This is what you must believe without reservation before you make any attempts at healing this devastating broken place.

Jarvis Williams, associate professor of New Testament Interpretation at the Southern Baptist Theological Seminary, was quoted in a recent article published in *Christianity Today*, laying it out clearly and succinctly:

> All kinds of racially and ethnically diverse people can be justified by faith in Christ (Rom. 3:21-4:25); repent of and turn from their sins (Acts 2:1-38); and be reconciled to God (Rom. 5:6-10) and to each other (Eph. 2:11-22). Throughout Scripture, we see that the gospel demands this diverse community intentionally to pursue one another in love (John 13:34-35; 1 John 2:10; 3:10-11, 14, 16, 18, 23; 4:7-12, 20-21). If churches desire to offer any help to those enslaved to racist ideologies, like the ones recently on display in Charlottesville, or to those who suffer from white supremacy, they must first see the gospel as the basis for our response.[59]

Look more carefully at this key passage:

> Together as one body, Christ reconciled both groups to God by means of His death on the cross, and our hostility toward each other was put to death. He brought this Good News of peace to you Gentiles who were far away from him, and peace to the Jews who were near. Now all of us can come to the Father through the same Holy Spirit because of what Christ has done for us.
>
> —Ephesians 2:16-18

Do you believe this and are you ready to rally behind it? If not, your efforts will not have the resources and power of Heaven behind them.

PUT TO DEATH SINFUL BELIEF PATTERNS
Clifton Clarke, associate dean of the William E. Pannell Center for African American Church Studies at Fuller Theological Seminary, in that same *Christianity Today* article cuts to the chase:

> The social and racial reconciliation we seek— and desperately need in America—comes at a cost: crucifying the sinful self."[60]

> My old self has been crucified with Christ. It is no longer I who live, but Christ lives in me. So I live in this earthly body by trusting in the Son of God, who loved me and gave himself for me.
>
> —Galatians 2:20

Racial reconciliation without such commitment merely provides a temporary Band-Aid to the problem. Talking about reconciliation in the face of events like Charlottesville is usually the first and only thing churches do, because it avoids the painful process of confronting the brutality of white privilege that continues to wreak havoc on black and brown lives. When asked if he would embrace white South Africans in a show of forgiveness during the apartheid era, a black South African remarked: 'How can I embrace you, when you're standing on my head?' Before any talk of reconciliation, according to theologian and minister Leonard Lovett, we need to begin with conciliation, the process to 'overcome the distrust or hostility.' There is no precedent for racial harmony in American history; we have to begin to create a world that is not predicated on white privilege, but on a common humanity.

RECOGNIZE, FACE, AND REPENT

I'm not sure where I saw this, but it makes total sense.

When you find yourself making an assumption about people, places, or things, challenge yourself by asking whether you know the assumption to be true, or if it is something you have simply been taught to believe by a racist society. Consider facts and evidence, especially those found in academic books and articles about race and racism rather than hearsay and "common sense."

"When you find yourself making an assumption about people, places, or things, challenge yourself by asking whether you know the assumption to be true, or if it is something you have simply been taught to believe by a racist society."

Acknowledge your biases. Admit your tendency to tribalism. Recognize how prone you are to be defensively ethnocentric. And confess your past and present racist actions.

Once you have done the hard, internal, soulish personal work, you can then begin to engage the world in a myriad of ways that will bring healing.

PARTNER WITH ORGANIZATIONS FIGHTING RACISM
Find local or national organizations that are deliberate in healing hatred. Support post-prison programs because the inflated incarceration rates of black and Latino people lead to their long-term economic and political disenfranchisement. And support community organizations that serve those bearing the mental, physical, and economic costs of racism.

Here, too, are a couple of wonderful international organizations worth your investigation that have as their mission the healing of hatred and racism.

- ALARM - African Leadership and Reconciliation Ministries is an African-led and African-based organization that focuses on equipping leaders with the skills and knowledge needed to truly transform their communities. ALARM was founded following the massive and horrific 1994 genocide in Rwanda. Serving in many post and current conflict regions in central-eastern Africa, ALARM pours their efforts into training and transforming communities through servant leadership and the Christian message of forgiveness and reconciliation. ALARM develops servant leaders in the African Church and community who reconcile and transform lives affected by conflict and injustice.[61]

- NAIM – North American Indigenous Ministries is an organization that works with native and non-native believers to reconcile Native Americans to Christ and His followers. This ministry thrives on Penelakut Island, British Columbia, a reservation overshadowed by a history of racism, abuse, and social injustice perpetuated in the name of Christ. Many of the locals suffered through the horrors of the Indian residential school system—a network of boarding schools for indigenous people created by the Canadian government and administered by Christian churches beginning in the late 1800s. The school system was created for the purpose of removing children from the influence of their own culture and assimilating them into the dominant Canadian culture. NAIM works to develop healthy relationships with the Penelakut people and invites them to experience the adventure of following Christ.[62]

PRAY AGAINST HATRED

I love these very practical prayer suggestions I discovered on a website of a Roman Catholic order, the Augustinians:

To the Creator of all races and peoples, who loves each of us for our uniqueness, we offer our prayers of petition: For an end to discrimination in all its forms, we pray ... Lord of all nations, hear our prayer.

That each person may be respected and valued as a child of God, we pray ... Lord of all nations, hear our prayer. That each of us may acknowledge our part in mistakes and sins of the past pertaining to discrimination and racism, we pray ... Lord of all nations, hear our prayer.

For a spirit of forgiveness and reconciliation among peoples who share a history of mutual mistrust, hatred or aggression, we pray ... Lord of all nations, hear our prayer.

That the victims of racial prejudice may forgive those who persecute them, and that their persecutors may have a change of heart, we pray ... Lord of all nations, hear our prayer.

For those who have struggled in the past and continue to do so today for civil rights, economic justice and the elimination of discrimination based on race, nationality or religion, we pray ... Lord of all nations, hear our prayer.

For the conversion of the hearts and minds of those who allow another's race to influence their relationships and limit their openness, we pray ... Lord of all nations, hear our prayer.

That we may work to influence the attitudes of others by expressly rejecting racial or ethnic stereotypes, slurs and jokes and be affirming of the cultural contributions of every racial, ethnic and religious group in our world, we pray ... Lord of all nations, hear our prayer.

That we may make a personal commitment to abolish social structures which inhibit economic, educational and social advancement of the poor, we pray ... Lord of all nations, hear our prayer.

That we may work for decent working conditions, adequate income, housing, education and health care for all people, we pray ... Lord of all nations, hear our prayer.[63]

In a *Christianity Today* article, Patricia Raybon suggests that if we want to see healing in racism and hatred we take a page out of Oswald Chambers' life and get on our knees! She says:

> Frustrated activists on both sides (including myself) may be inclined to skip this step. When race matters confound us, our biggest deficit, Chambers would argue, is in our prayer lives. "We do not pray at all," he said, "until we are at our wit's end." As he famously said, "Prayer does not equip us for greater works—prayer *is* the greater work. As believers, we know this in theory, of course. But Chambers invites us to let go in practice—to pray to God first, not for solutions but for *him*. We don't pray to get hold of answers, says Chambers, we pray "to get hold of God."

She concludes with this prophetic word: "This is a deeply needed challenge for the church universal, but especially for evangelicalism in America, a system still draped in sorrowing racial baggage. By praying with more intent, however, God's people love with more abandon. 'If my heart is right with God,' says Chambers, 'every human being is my neighbor.'"[64]

In very practical terms, you might want to create a prayer journal or notebook or scrapbook to chronicle your prayers for the end of hatred. Or, form a prayer team around the issue of hatred. Perhaps you should take the point in creating a multi-racial, multi-ethnic city-wide prayer movement to deal with hatred and racism.

BECOME A PUBLIC ADVOCATE

Here are a number of ways you can become a public advocate for the end of hatred.

- Stop your coworker or relative or friend when they make that racist comment. Call out hatred and racism even when it is uncomfortable. If you see something, say something. Step in when you see racism occurring, and disrupt it in a safe way. Have hard conversations with others when you hear or see racism, whether explicit or implicit. Challenge racist assumptions by asking about supporting facts and evidence (in general, they do not exist). Have conversations about what led you and/or others to have racist beliefs.

- Listen to, validate, and ally with people who report personal and systemic racism. Take claims of racism seriously.

- Learn about the racism that occurs where you live, and do something about it by participating in and supporting anti-racist community events, protests, rallies, and programs.

- Communicate with your local and state government officials and institutions about how they can help end racism in the communities they represent.

- Support voter registration and polling in neighborhoods where people of color live because they have historically been marginalized in the political process.

Here are a few other ideas taken from *11 Things White People Can Do to Be Real Anti-Racist Allies:*

- "Ask your black or Asian friend what books they'd recommend you read. It will probably be received a lot better than asking them to explain race to you right then and there." — Arthur Chu

- "Look at your relationship with language. Every time you are texting, tweeting or Facebooking, you are making choices about words and the stories you tell about race. I try to raise awareness that we're trafficking in racial ideology 24-7 online—and that we can change the direction of these conversations every time we hit "comment." — Daisy Hernández

- "Get up and protest. Understandably, protests are inaccessible to many, but there are other options. I'm a firm believer in DIY activism, and it's something with which I am actively involved. Create something—zines, art, podcasts, articles." — Sarah Sahim[65]

EDUCATE YOUR KIDS
We have an obligation to our children to raise them to love others and respect differences. This should start as soon as they are gifted to you, but it's never too late to instill this message in them. I don't need to add to what Jen Wang says about how we do that:

> If you have children, even very young children, talk to them about race. Don't wait until they encounter a problem at school, among friends, or hear about something in the news to engage them on the subject of difference. Teach them that multiculturalism and diversity aren't just about food, costumes, holidays, and having a few brown faces in a classroom to break up the whiteness. Expose them to books, TV and movies featuring people of color as protagonists and heroes.[66]

GET IN THE ROOM AND STAY IN THE ROOM
This phrase, "Get in the room and stay in the room," stuck with me ever since my friend Jim Henderson came up with it. I'll return to this in the next chapter on SEPARATION; but, simply put, it means to enter into relationship with folks and don't run away when things get tough or contentious.

"Get in the room and stay in the room"

"Will you question who you choose to befriend and who you choose to ignore in your daily interactions, and think how race might play a part?" Sam Sanders, NPR[67]

"Stop talking for a minute and just listen: Comparing the situation of a person of color to some personal anecdote of yours is not as constructive as you think it is. Do not think that your innate wisdom or some personal experience has prepared you for a discussion. Do some research before trying to engage in a conversation, preferably written by a person of color. And, for the love of god, stop asking about our hair."— Kara Brown, staff writer, *Jezebel*[68]

Cross the racial divide (and other sources of division) by offering friendly greetings to people, regardless of race, gender, age, sexuality, ability, class, or housing status. Think about who you make eye contact with, nod to, or say "Hello" to while you are out in the world. If you notice a pattern of preference and exclusion, shake it up. Respectful, friendly, everyday communication is the essence of community.

Learn Spanish or Arabic or French or any other language to allow you to become engaged deeply in relationship.

In America, it's a national indictment that 75 percent of white Americans don't have any close non-white friends, according to 2016 findings by the Public Religion Research Institute. Religious insularity is a problem, too. A lack of knowing people outside one's racial and religious box—seems tough to overcome but critical to correct.

You, Again

I want to remind you of the quote with which I opened Chapter One: "We were built to count, as water is made to run downhill. We are placed in a specific context to count in ways no one else does. That is our destiny.[69] "

You are a masterpiece, created, perhaps, for such a time as this. Right in the middle of this civil war at the intersection of hate and history.

If your heart is stirred by this chapter on the broken place of HATRED then it may be that your God-given destiny is wrapped up in healing it! But know this, it will take an activist's heart and will. Activists are insurgents. Activists are revolutionaries. And activists get attacked.

But, you know that, don't you? And, I know what you're thinking: *Bring it on!*

CHAPTER 7
AMBASSADORS

If we find ourselves with a desire that nothing in this world can satisfy, the most probable explanation is that we were made for another world.
— C.S. Lewis

I lay in my bed in my dirty college apartment in absolute misery. Sick with a bad case of mononucleosis along with my ever-present chronic anxiety-induced nausea. Worried . . . no, more like frantic . . . since I had blown off so many classes, too ill to attend. Frustrated that my dreams of going to med school were disappearing fast; lonely, afraid, lost.

I was very lost, which would not make sense to most people who had observed the previous twenty years of my life. I was a church guy—the one who was faithful to attend worship, proud I could speedily find any book of the Bible, and quick to *appear* "holy." I looked the part of the dutiful Christian.

Except that I wasn't. I was lost. I was very much separated from the God of the universe. I was Christian in name only.

I had memorized this passage of Scripture as a child: "Anyone who belongs to Christ has become a new person. The old life is gone; a new life has begun!" (2 Corinthians 5:17) Well, that wasn't me. No new life had ever begun in me. Never had I "belonged" to God. My old life was still my only life.

And it was a miserable, duplicitous life. Good boy on the outside/ugly boy on the inside, controlled by dark immoral thoughts and actions. And there was no notion whatsoever of calling or destiny. I just thought being a doctor would be cool. Of course, that idea was shot anyway.

Did I tell you how lost I was?

Then something happened. Something that came kinda out of the blue. Maybe from my desperate heart? From God's gracious grip on me? Both? As I lay in that bed, drapes drawn, sheets up to my chin, tears flowing down my cheeks, I cried out to God. I think I said something like this (out loud), "God, if you are real, and all the stuff I was taught is true, and you can forgive me . . . I surrender my life to you."

Nothing happened.

Well, not immediately. But in the ensuing weeks, it was clear that I had crossed some rubicon—some point of no return—and I began to experience a transformation that had eluded me in all my Sunday School years.

And, then, literally within weeks of that, I had my own Ephesians 2:10 moment in which my calling became wonderfully clear.

Nope, God didn't call me to be a doctor. He called me to be a pastor.

So, why tell you my story? Well, because I represented the typical American then and today. The overwhelming majority of people in the US (between 70 and 80 percent) claim some kind of affiliation with God or Jesus. But most are as lost as the day is long. As lost as I was. They are Christian in name only and absolutely separated from the God of the universe. I'll bet they are miserable, too. And if not miserable, they are confused and looking for some direction for their not-so-great lives.

I know some of you wonder about this. You might be thinking, *I don't know if I buy that.* Maybe you've never been convinced that most human beings exist in a state of alienation from God. Shoot, let's be honest, maybe you're not even so sure about the existence of God, period. At the very least, even if you are indeed a theist (one who believes in the existence of God, but not a God who is actively working in our lives) you might struggle with a belief that insists that mankind requires a savior.

Finally, even *if* you buy all that, the idea of healing separation through evangelism just terrifies you or frustrates you or makes you roll your eyes. Evangelism—the art and practice of persuading another to surrender their life to Jesus—might be, to you, at best daunting. It can feel *really* politically incorrect.

> "All the brokenness of the world found in PAIN, DECAY, ISOLATION, HATRED, and INJUSTICE has its roots in this prime broken place of SEPARATION."

So, all that said, I know it might be hard to maintain your interest till the end of this last broken place. But, may I ask that you suspend your concerns for a few moments and hear me out? Because herein lies the source of *all* the other broken places. SEPARATION from God is the granddaddy of all the rest. If we do not get this one right, then any attempts at healing the other five, though heroic and beautiful, might just be Band-Aids. All the brokenness of the world found in PAIN, DECAY, ISOLATION, HATRED, and INJUSTICE has its roots in this prime broken place of SEPARATION.

The scope and scale of this broken place is astonishing and daunting. And the impact or effect of the separation from God on individuals, families, friendships, cultures, and nations is undeniable.

Let me give you three glaringly obvious examples.

First, let me repeat. I know I risk overstating my point, but I think I've made it clear in the preceding chapters just how badly PAIN, ISOLATION, INJUSTICE, DECAY, and HATRED have destroyed the good and abundant life we all long for. Again, this is the case *because* humans are separated from God, continue to sin, and "everybody does what is right in their own eyes." (Judges 21:25). We are sliding back to the bottom of the barrel of human willful, ignorant rebellion that led God at one point in human history to say, "I am sorry I ever made them," because he "observed the extent of human wickedness on the earth, and saw that everything humans thought or imagined was consistently and totally evil." (Genesis 6:5-6)

Could our separation from him be drawing us back to the bottom?

Another obvious effect of our alienation from God is our overall state of morality. And by morality, I mean our ethics and our standards of right and wrong that play out in our behavior. I know that many would take issue with my suggestion of an increase in human wickedness. Here's an example. In a HuffPost article written in May of 2017, John Pavlovitz said the idea that "this country is in moral decline . . . made him more than a bit nauseous." He calls the fear of moral decline a pining for "ol' time religion." Mr. Pavlovitz goes on:

> This idea of our country's present moral decay has become a go-to Evangelical Christian trope for decades; an attempt at a literal self-fulfilling prophecy, where the world is falling hopelessly apart, and the Church is the lone,

faithful remnant standing in the face of the heathen culture's rebellion. Much like Noah, these religious people imagine themselves sole builders of the only safe place from God's coming wrath; the waters of dread surely and swiftly rising. But the truth is America is not in decline any more than at any time in its history. This is just lazy religious-speak.[70]

Now, I happen to agree with most of what Mr. Pavlovitz has to say but, no, I do not agree with him or anyone who might suggest that we are not in a time of moral decline. Immorality is not a trope. It is an ugly literal thing. Let me suggest just three moral dives we are experiencing right now.

We lie like we've never lied before. I don't need stats for this. You know. I know. We are living in a time of "alternative facts." One writer recently said, "The sheer shameless magnitude of lies is unprecedented in world history."[71] Twentieth century political theorist Hannah Arendt warned of the impact of such a preponderance of untruth. "The result of a consistent and total substitution of lies for factual truth is not that the lies will now be accepted as truth . . . but that the sense by which we take our bearings in the real world . . . is being destroyed."[72]

Then there's aberrant sexual behavior. I can't help it, but after decades of listening to hundreds of confessions of infidelity, enduring too many revelations of internet porn addiction, and being repulsed by dozens of horrendous stories of sexual abuse, etc., etc., etc., etc., ad nauseum (literally), I am here to tell you our sexual morality has never been worse. Disagree? Google it. No, don't Google it.

And finally, abortion. Annually around 900,000 babies are aborted each year in the US alone. The United States is eclipsed in abortions by only nine other countries worldwide. Those numbers are stunning whether or not you believe it is wrong. I believe it is evidence of a "lostness" in human beings that would cause or allow such devastation to human souls— the mother's, the father's, and of course the child's.

It is glaringly obvious to me that our separation from God is causing outrageous moral decline. And I haven't even mentioned the increase of substance abuse, fraud, corruption, bullying, rage, gluttony, hedonism, greed, pride, and on, and on, and on. Billions of human beings are separated from God, and as a result, we are falling into a black hole of moral indecency.

But immorality is not the only sign of separation from God. Without spiritual moorings, without divine guidance, without the love of the eternal Father, humans are wallowing in debilitating chronic anxiety. Not knowing who to turn to, we fret, fuss, worry, and emotionally fall apart. This then leads to, as Edwin Friedman describes in his excellent book *A Failure of Nerve,* these societal characteristics: reactivity, herding, and blame displacement.[73] In our separation from God and resultant deep anxiety, we point fingers. We gather people around us who agree with us, and attack the leaders who are trying to rescue us. I have to be honest, I despair over the furious, anxiety-dominated rage that is besetting our world. It is provoking evil. And that evil is ripping society apart.

Again, it's obvious to me we are suffering from separation from God. And one more thing. Despite the increase of those who profess no religious affiliation, the perceived rise of atheism and the watering down of true faith among those who claim affinity with Jesus, people are still hungry for someone or something beyond themselves. This has been a constant concern of mine through all my decades of pastoral work. People need God and want God and acutely feel their alienation from him. Even young men and women, expressing their discomfort with status quo religion (I don't blame them), sigh wistfully, realizing they still want to believe in *something*! Ravi Zacharias, well-known Christian apologist, would agree. "After nearly three decades of crisscrossing the globe and lecturing at numerous campuses around the world, it is evident to me that the yearning for the spiritual just will not die. In fact, at virtually every engagement I have found the auditorium filled to capacity and the appreciative response quite overwhelming, even in antagonistic settings."[74]

So, yeah. It's obvious to me. Humanity is separated from God. This is the core broken place of the world. Zacharias also says, "Though proud skepticism is rife in academic bastions, the human spirit still longs for something more. This tension must be addressed, especially at this time of cultural upheaval. Here the greatest question of our time must be considered: Can man live without God?"[75]

Beginning with the story of Adam and Eve and on through the latest acts of rebellion today, men and women have willfully, stupidly, and many times, ignorantly chosen to distance themselves from the God of the universe. Call it what you will—sin, transgression, or immorality—the misdeeds of people have led to their estrangement from God. Here it is - short and not-so-sweet.

For everyone has sinned; we all fall short of God's glorious standard.

—Romans 3:23

And in falling short of God's standard for us, we suffer immeasurably. Here's just a short list from the Scriptures of the ramifications of this separation from God, this originator of all broken places.

Because we are separated from God we are:

- *separated from the life of God (Ephesians 4:18),*

- *living "without hope" (Ephesians 2:12),*

- *experiencing "the hidden face of God" (Isaiah 59:2),*

- *struggling with "hard hearts" (Ephesians 4:18),*

- *living daily in "ignorance" and "darkened under-standing" (Ephesians 4:18).*

Or perhaps, more simply and to the point, we are "lost" (Luke 19:10) and "dead" (Ephesians 2:1).

It's quite stunning, isn't it, to see in print that which we know in our hearts? No wonder people are so messed up! But, in God's mercy, He provided a way for reconciliation to occur with His dearly loved people.

> When we were utterly helpless, Christ came at just the right time and died for us sinners. Now, most people would not be willing to die for an upright person, though someone might perhaps be willing to die for a person who is especially good. But God showed his great love for us by sending Christ to die for us while we were still sinners.
>
> —Romans 5:6-8

And that reconciliation—the end of the separation—occurs when each individual human being, by faith, surrenders their life to Jesus.

> For this is how God loved the world: He gave his one and only Son, so that everyone who believes in him will not perish but have eternal life.
>
> —John 3:16

> But to all who believed him and accepted him, he gave the right to become children of God. They are reborn—not with a physical birth resulting from human passion or plan, but a birth that comes from God.
>
> —John 1:12-13

Much more could be said, of course. But this is the essence of God's view on our separation from him and the remedy for that separation.

There is one more thing. The remedy, the healing, of this particular broken place, will occur when individuals humbly and with deep repentance accept the state of their souls before God and commence the act of surrender to Jesus. But, for the vast majority of people who do surrender, who are saved, who are reconciled with God, they do not get there on their own. They need help, guidance, provocation, and many times, convincing. So, like all the other broken places, this one requires great effort. In the same way you will have to adjust your life to engage deeply in the healing of INJUSTICE, with the same passion rising within you to end HATRED, with the same commitment required to engage in the DECAY of the planet, you must determine to willfully engage in healing this broken place of SEPARATION. This is God's great desire and intention: that we become his messengers—His AMBASSADORS—of reconciliation!

What Is an Ambassador?

Jesus couldn't have been clearer as to what it will take to heal the broken place of SEPARATION.

> Therefore, go and make disciples of all the na-
> tions baptizing them in the name of the Father
> and the Son and the Holy Spirit. Teach these
> new disciples to obey all the commands I have
> given you. And be sure of this: I am with you
> always, even to the end of the age.
> —Matthew 28:19-20

and

> You will receive power when the Holy Spirit
> comes upon you. And you will be my witnesses,
> telling people about me everywhere—in Jerusa-
> lem, throughout Judea, in Samaria, and to the
> ends of the earth.
> —Acts 1:8

Jesus indicates that to heal the separation of people from God it would take deliberateness on the part of his followers. Determination to go, a resolve to pass on his teaching, and the tenacity to provoke lost people to surrender to Christ. It would also require a willingness to pursue lost people as far as was needed, even to "the ends of the earth."

A number of years following this challenge or commission Jesus made to his followers, the Apostle Paul gave a title to those who would go and make disciples of Jesus. He called them AMBASSADORS.

> Christ gave us this wonderful message of reconciliation. So we are his ambassadors; God is making his appeal through us. We speak for Christ when we plead, 'Come back to God!"
>
> —2 Corinthians 5:17 20

Maybe you are better acquainted with the term in a governmental sense. So, what do ambassadors do? They go to different areas of the globe and represent the interests of those who sent them. They cultivate relationships in an effort to be able to help others understand the leader they represent. So, in evangelism, ambassadors engage in the art of helping another to see their life through the lens of Jesus and his teaching and persuade them to surrender to him.

Now, don't mistake this role as one that is best left to the professionals, i.e. pastors and missionaries. No, this responsibility is shared by all those who claim Jesus as their Lord and Savior.

> If someone asks about your hope as a believer, always be ready to explain it.
>
> —1 Peter 3:15

Ambassadors: Healers of Separation

Hang around someone who is worked up about INJUSTICE and you'll hear their indignation over vast systems of tragedy and unfairness. Spend time with a NURTURER and you'll catch their broken heart for lonely people. Hang out with a person concerned about the DECAY of the planet and you'll likely be taught the wonders of vegetarianism and recycling. Sit with a HEALER and you'll feel a visceral concern for suffering folk. Follow an ACTIVIST around and you'll get caught up in their fervor against racism. Get alongside an AMBASSADOR and you'll know right away they are on a holy quest with eternal consequences.

Here's a case in point. In my lifetime, no one exemplified the heart of an AMBASSADOR like the late Billy Graham. The world's foremost evangelist for close to seven decades, Billy lived with a passion born out of a destiny that affected millions of people. Here's what he said shortly before he died:

> I hope I will be remembered as someone who was faithful—faithful to God, faithful to the Gospel of Jesus Christ and faithful to the calling God gave me not only as an evangelist, but as a husband, father and friend.
>
> I'm sure I've failed in many ways, but I take comfort in Christ's promise of forgiveness, and I take comfort also in God's ability to take even our most imperfect efforts and use them for His glory.
>
> By the time you read this, I will be in Heaven, and as I write this I'm looking forward with great anticipation to the day when I will be in God's presence forever.

I'm convinced that Heaven is far more glorious than anything we can possibly imagine right now, and I look forward not only to its wonder and peace, but also to the joy of being reunited with those who have gone there before me, especially my dear wife, Ruth. The Bible says, "Now we see but a poor reflection as in a mirror; then we shall see face to face" (1 Corinthians 13:12).

But I won't be in Heaven because I've preached to large crowds or because I've tried to live a good life. I'll be in Heaven for one reason: Many years ago I put my faith and trust in Jesus Christ, who died on the cross to make our forgiveness possible and rose again from the dead to give us eternal life. Do you know you will go to heaven when you die? You can, by committing your life to Jesus Christ today.

"For God so loved the world that he gave his one and only Son, that whoever believes in him shall not perish but have eternal life" (John 3:16).

Put your trust in Christ today.[76]

So, do you think you can be an AMBASSADOR? If you believe that Jesus offers the greatest remedy to the broken place of SEPARATION, then you are already equipped. All it takes is the conviction to share the hope and healing you have received. But, as with ACTIVISTS, there is stigma attached to this healer role. You may be characterized as a "Holy Roller," a "Bible Thumper," or as judgmental, exclusionary, or religious nut. That goes with the territory of speaking from your convictions. But if you step into your role as an AMBASSADOR, operating solely from a place of love for your fellow human beings, seeking to restore them to relationship with their creator, offering them a way to navigate life with hope and purpose, you can reach people more effectively.

Let me introduce you to a few folks—AMBASSADORS who get this and who have devoted their lives to healing this broken place.

CATHY FOLEY

The best healers are the ones who have experienced healing themselves. There is a certain "pay it forward" passion that is exuded by one who knows what it feels like to experience brokenness and then relief. When it comes to separation from God, that is Cathy Foley's story. She told me, "I identify with people who aren't whole. I have deep empathy for people who are separated from God." This is because that's where she found herself while facing what she calls "seven great years of tribulation."

Interestingly, before surrendering her life to Jesus, Cathy was no pagan. In fact, she was quite religious and gave everyone the impression that all was right between her and God. She describes herself as being, at one time, very "compliant—living by a clear moral check list." She often spoke publicly about her faith and was even called a "Bible banger" by some in her church. But, this belied what was going on inside of her.

Cathy told me, "I didn't really know what it meant to follow Jesus. Mostly I wandered spiritually 'by feel.' I tried to intellectualize my faith but didn't get it." Then came her seven years of great tribulation. Her marriage fell into great distress and eventually ended in divorce. She faced deep struggles with her children. And then came the diagnosis of breast cancer. Tribulation indeed.

It was in this very tough time that Cathy began to "face her pain and to hear God!" She says, "I realized I couldn't function on my own wherewithal. The Bible began to come alive! The whole experience brought me close to the living God. And I realized that he was there for me."

It was on the heels of this personal renewal that she felt God start to encourage her to share her joy and faith with others. Cathy reflects on that time: "I feel like God said to me 'Tell them out of your mouth!" Reflecting on her interactions with other women facing issues similar to hers, especially separation from God, she felt God say, *Tell her she is precious. Tell her you are his treasure.*

This has become part of her calling. She told me, "I always seem to have people around me, begging me, "Tell me your story." Cathy knows part of her destiny is to lead people to be reconciled to God through Jesus.

Cathy's job had put her in proximity to people from all over the world. It was not unusual for me to look down and see her sitting on the front row of church with someone she'd invited and connected with at work. I have had the joy of baptizing, with Cathy, a young woman from China who found Jesus as a result of meeting and being led to God through Cathy. Side note: that young woman now emulates her mentor, Cathy, and is quite a force for Jesus in her home country.

Cathy is one of the most exuberant people I know! These days she is cancer free, remarried to a wonderful husband, Bob, and is enjoying a renewed relationship with her children and grandchildren. But what will never change is her deep commitment to persuade others to know and love God. It is her destiny to heal the broken place of SEPARATION!

HEATH SHANER

Heath is a smart young man. He's one of those kids that makes an impression on you right off . . . looks you in the eye as he shakes your hand and tells you what a pleasure it is to talk with you. Heath is fifteen years old, and boy, is he smart, and wow, does he love God!

But he didn't always. A few years ago, Heath hated going to church. Maybe it was his wrestling over the fact that he almost died as a child or that his grandpa passed away too soon, but Heath was quite unsure about God. But something his grandpa told him rattled him enough to do something about his lack of faith. "You gotta get your stuff together!" is what his grandfather said.

And he did. Heath threw himself into researching the viability of his faith. He began studying theology and researching the claims of Jesus. He's read more books on apologetics than I have ever read! He is now a passionate believer and ambassador for God! He told me, "Jesus said to go and make disciples of all nations. I just kind of take that to heart. I just realize what God has done in my life and in some of my friends and family members. I know what my life was like without God, so I just do everything in my power that I can to get people to come to Christ!"

Despite his winsomeness and relational skills, Heath is careful to deflect any admiration. "Ultimately, my end goal is to give God the glory. If it wasn't for God's intervention in my life, I wouldn't be the person that I am today. If I would have not listened to his calling, I wouldn't be the person I am today."

When this kid talks about God, it's with intelligence and grace. He says, "I'm not a Bible thumper, but I like to use practical reasons to help people out and get them to know Christ." And he can be insistent!

He said, "I plant stones in peoples' shoes", making people wrestle with what they believe. And when they ask . . . he's there with an answer!

Did I tell you that Heath is fifteen years old?

OTHER AMBASSADORS

While researching this chapter I asked some of my friends and co-workers if they could identify other ambassadors, people who were passionate about healing the broken place of SEPARATION. I was looking for a few good stories like Cathy and Heath. I was blown away at the number of amazing people they pointed me too. And I was intrigued at what motivated those folks to do the hard thing of helping others be reconciled to the God of the universe. Here's some of what they said. I asked them:

Why are you concerned that people be made right with God... or why are you an ambassador for God?

Laurie Sole – "Because God tells us to reach others. He left us to do that job and trying to live my life doing what he wants is important to me. Also, when I think of people living without the benefit of knowing Jesus it makes me sad."

Ted Eads – "A personal experience shaped my perspective on working with others to find the love and hope in Jesus. When

I was fifteen years old, I was living in a home with a verbally and abusive father. I do not believe that I had ever in my life felt safe. I did attend church growing up, but because of my circumstance, I questioned if God was real. Although I had questions, I prayed often to be rescued from the life situation I was in. I felt hopeless. In the summer of 1978, I ended up in our basement with a gun to my head believing that I had found the answer and escape route. I can tell you that the Holy Spirit is real. I heard the Spirit that day telling me that it would be ok, that He loved me. I listened. I listened. I listened. These are reasons why I have strong feelings that we must share the love of our God. With him, we can find joy in the darkness and pain of life."

Ty Tancredi – "I'm able, with my horrible prior life of addiction to drugs, to connect with people who are down. I fully believe I'm destined to bring good news to everyone who is broken because I've been there. If Jesus can overcome my addiction he can overcome anything you have too! When you know you're loved by God, it changes everything."

Heather Hughes - "I desire so deeply to share these truths with people who do not know him because I want to see their burdens lifted. I think a lot of people forget that he is living - like alive and involved and wanting so desperately to walk with them, to help them, to carry the weight for them. I cannot imagine going through day to day challenges let alone a serious life event without the hope of God's promises - that he is always there."

Jon Hughes - "The world we live in is broken. We experience pain, death, loss, hurt, hardship, illness, and all manner of destruction around us. However, when even one surrenders to Jesus and is reconciled with God, it represents the potential to make a change to the brokenness."

How do you go about practicing evangelism?

Heather Hughes – "Relationships. Authenticity. Vulnerability. Food. Play dates. Work outs. Always being willing to go there."

Jon Hughes - "I join others in acknowledging my own brokenness. As humans we share many like experiences, and, unfortunately, one of those is pain. When I share the pain of my own life, it gives me the opportunity to share the hope and healing Jesus has brought to me."

Ty Tancredi – "I lay hands on sick people and sometimes just lend an ear to listen, so that when I do evangelize, our hearts are in sync with God's heart for people to be saved!"

Laurie Sole – "I look for the way depending on the person. Some people need to be wooed. Some need relationship with us, some need years, some need love and compassion, some need prayer and "hands off". . . . I can be bold at times and hold back at others but if I stay close to the Holy Spirit and listen, I usually know which way to go with someone."

Ted Eads – "I share my faith by living it. I also spend a good amount of time listening! It seems to be my theme."

These people live their faith and bleed their faith and speak their faith. And all around them the broken place of SEPARATION is being healed.

How to Step into Your Ambassador Calling

The first step on the *Path of Yes* to your destiny as an AMBASSADOR might be a literal one to a neighbor's home. It might be an invitation to coffee. Or a note dropped in the mail. The first steps on the road to healing SEPARATION almost always include the start of a conversation. And it is in those moments of dialogue that lost human beings begin to feel the love of God, perhaps for the first time. From you!

Does the SEPARATION of human beings from God leave you frustrated? Does the lostness of your friends and family make your heart hurt? Does it cause you despair that so many are so far from God? Then let's talk about some ways you could be part of the solution. Your God-given destiny may very well be wrapped up in the souls of others! The impact of your calling could last far, far beyond these earthly days and stretch into eternity!

A reminder though. You will have to choose *brave, not safe*. The costs are significant. It will take time . . . lots of time and patience. It might also lead to deep levels of frustration and disappointment as the people you love want nothing to do with your faith. You will despair watching men and women reject the God you believe in. You will throw your hands up in exasperation as people choose an empty life again and again.

But it's worth it. You know it is. It's worth the contempt and sadness because of the spectacular moments of joy and exhilaration when one person turns to God and is healed. It is all worth it when you get to be the one who leads the prodigal back home to the Father.

The thought of that is all you need! Right?

PRACTICE THE ART OF EVANGELISM

Yes, there are other ways you can be a part of bringing healing to the broken place of SEPARATION other than evangelism. You could find ways to partner with ministries and organizations that have evangelism as their core mission. Cru, Intervarsity, and Young Life are just a few that come to mind. Like every other faith-based organization, they are anxious to find volunteers to support them in a myriad of ways, especially financially. But until an army of people, including you, determine to do this thing—become an ambassador of the gospel and practice evangelism—this broken place will remain hopelessly broken.

> "We must, must, must, get in this game. Kindly, lovingly, but with great intention, we must be deliberate in our attempts to lovingly convince others to surrender to Jesus."

We must, must, must, get in *this* game. Kindly, lovingly, but with great intention, we must be deliberate in our attempts to lovingly convince others to surrender to Jesus.

How can your family member ever find Jesus unless you lead him there? How will your classmates in school have a ghost of a chance of finding God unless you tell them how? How will your neighbor discover the incredible new and eternal life possible for them unless *somebody* introduces them to it?

We must take people by the hand and show them that God loves them. We must open up spiritual conversations with the people in our spheres of influence. We have no choice. The world will slide further into misery the more we fold our arms and pretend it's okay to be separated from God. I think you get my point.

So, if you want to know how to become adept at the practice of evangelism, read on.

There are many excellent books on this subject, so there really is no need for me to reinvent the wheel. As a matter of fact, perhaps the first thing you should do if you want to get engaged in healing the broken place of SEPARATION is to read some of these writings. Here are two you might want to consider:

Evangelism Without Additives by Jim Henderson.

I Once Was Lost by Don Everts and Doug Schaupp

Particularly enlightening in Everts and Schaupp's book is their understanding of the thresholds each person must cross to move from lack of faith to surrender to Jesus. Another way they characterize this journey of faith is the movement through five distinct seasons of growth.

They are:

- from distrust to trust,
- from complacent to curious,
- from closed to open to change,
- from meandering to seeking,
- from seeking to crossing into the Kingdom (relationship with God).

Everts and Schaupp suggest that this journey is both mysterious and organic. "To admit that is liberation. The monkey is off our back, and onto God's back, where it belongs."[77] In other words, as a person comes to faith it is a "soulish" journey that can't be treated as linear or as a simple transaction.

That said, there are indeed determined efforts you can make to practice loving evangelism that will nudge and guide a person along in their faith development (and not turn them off along the way!).

FIRST, BE CREDIBLE

In the post-Christian world we inhabit, so much of Christianity is simply not credible, believable or trustworthy any more.

- The Bible is not credible.
- The church is not credible.
- Christians are not credible.
- God is not credible (nor Jesus).
- Our dogmatic truth is not credible.

In his book *Meet Generation Z*, James Emery White quotes political strategist Doug Sosnick: "The United States is going through the most significant period of change since the beginning of the industrial revolution."[78] White describes this change as more than simply secularism; it's really functional atheism. "Rather than rejecting the idea of God, our culture simply ignores him."[79] He quotes Kathy Lynn Grossman, the co-researcher of the famed 2008 American Religious Identification Survey: "People are not thinking about religion and rejecting it; they're not thinking about it at all." This ethos has led to the rise of the fastest growing faith group in America, the "nones"—those who, when asked to identify a faith group to which they belong would say "none."

So, credibility . . . your credibility . . . as an ambassador of God is key.

Here is another way to look at it: Early on in my own faith journey I was taught that there is a gap between human beings and God caused by sin. And the way over that chasm was through faith in Jesus Christ. I was shown this in illustration form on many a napkin or piece of scrap paper. It looked something like this:

People (Sinful)   **God (Holy)**

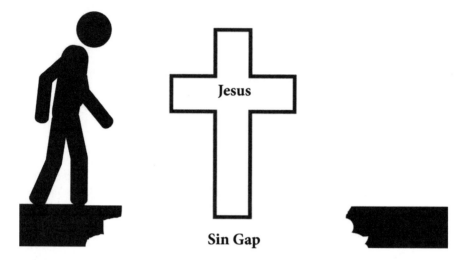

Today we need an updated version of this illustration. There are now two gaps. And, as is demonstrated in this updated version, a person won't even have a slim chance of considering their separation from God until they cross the first gap—the credibility gap. And the way over that first, most difficult, gap is you. You must be credible.

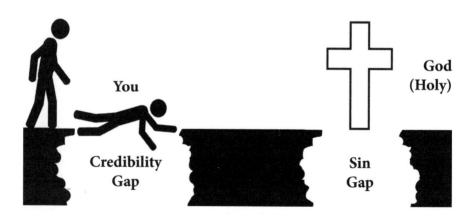

How does an AMBASSADOR of God become credible or trustworthy or believable? Jim Henderson does a wonderful job of encouraging credibility in our lives in *Evangelism without Additives.*

Jim suggests we first learn how to pay attention:

> People crave attention. In our cultural setting it's like the cup of cold water Jesus referred to in Matthew 10:42, where he said, 'If anyone gives even a cup of cold water to one of these little ones because he is my disciple . . . he will certainly not lose his reward.' When we pay attention to people because we want to nudge them toward Jesus, it refreshes them. It becomes the connecting bridge between them and God. Best of all, instead of asking them for something—*their* time, attention, and interest—we give them something—*our* time, attention, and interest. We serve them a small taste of Jesus's desire to attend to them.[80] (emphasis mine)

I love that Jim goes one step further and suggests that we be "unusually interested" in others. This is the first, most important way we can "lay down" over the credibility gap. When a person knows that you genuinely are interested in them, they will begin to open themselves to you and slowly move from distrust to trust.

Now, to help them over the next two thresholds—from complacent to curious and from closed to open to change—it's going to take a lot of normal conversation. As Henderson suggests, "Forget the speech, the pitch, and the program." Be normal. "Normal people are the ones who get the important things done."[81] And when the time seems right, mix in your own story of connecting with God. If you have been unusually interested in them and if you hang out with people in normal ways, opportunities for spiritual conversations will happen naturally. And when they do, go there!

But, there may come a hitch. Your friend may, at some point react, take issue, disagree, or make it uncomfortable to continue the conversation. Remember, they have huge credibility issues with just about everything you hold dear. When that happens let me suggest, again, what Jim Henderson recommends. When you get in the room, stay in the room. Stick it out. Be patient. Listen. As Everts and Schaupp suggest, "Don't avoid. Don't judge. Don't argue. And even look for opportunities to affirm."[82] If you don't run when they push back, they'll likely listen when you return to the conversation in the future. Stay in the room.

Now, should your friend progress to the point of meandering, they are likely going to need some intentionality on your part. To get them to truly seek the answers for their life you'll have to take some risks to push them a bit, mostly by asking good questions. Jesus did this all the time. Here are a few questions that might move them from spiritually meandering to a season of seeking:

- What is your take on the whole God question?
- What do you think life is about?
- Do you think you have a destiny?
- What is the most significant thing that has hap-pened to you in the last month?[83]

BE CURIOUS

So, let's assume that your friend has crossed the credibility gap (thanks to your humility and love) and has begun to seek.

How do you move them from seeking to "crossing over" into relationship with God? This is where an appropriate sense of urgency is required.

> Ask them clearly without oversimplifying if they are willing to surrender their life to Jesus. If they say no ask them why. Find out what their remaining questions are and what their blocks may be. Honestly help them resolve those barriers. Help them focus on Jesus and not on doctrine. Study the life of Jesus with them from the Gospels. And pray. And stay in the room. And continue to be unusually interested in them. And wait. And when the time seems right . . . gently go at it again.[84]

BE BALANCED

This whole thing of evangelism—healing the broken place of SEPARATION—requires great balance.

Brian McLaren, in the foreword to Jim's book, reflects on the two extremes of evangelism. He suggests first we must avoid being the "overconfident, argumentative, pushy, insensitive, and domineering Christian trying to 'witness' to someone. At the same time, we can't be the deeply afraid Christian who doesn't want to be judgmental and hurt someone so keeps their faith to themselves and never shares it with anyone."[85]

Rick Mattson in his book, *Faith is Like Skydiving*, warns us to "find the passive-active balance. If you trust God but don't speak, you're too passive. If you speak but don't trust God you're too active and your words will be impotent. Do both. Develop a plan, talk, witness, strive, love, argue."[86]

You, Again

Don't forget this. Don't *ever* forget this. You are God's masterpiece created with a calling and even a destiny in mind. Before you were born he, for sure, loved you, but he also liked you and saw *huge* potential in you to join him in his daily, hourly work of healing the 6 Broken Places of this world. So, which did he make you to be?

Are you a CHAMPION for JUSTICE? A NURTURER of love and connection? A HEALER of PAIN? A STEWARD of the creation? An ACTIVIST against hate? Or are you an AMBASSADOR to lead others to God?

Can you be more than one? Heck, yeah! Whatever your calling or destiny, throw yourself into it! Live brave, not safe!

Find your why to live for, and go make the earth shake where you walk!

CHAPTER 8
FINDING YOUR
DESTINY

*"If God gives you something you can do, why in God's name
wouldn't you do it?"*
— Stephen King

Destiny is such an epic word isn't it? It's intriguing. And it's
enticing. It makes you want to dream. And it can make you
cry. I've seen a lot of grown men and women weep over it.
Why?

Well, social scientists and psychologists will tell you
that we have a "tendency to actualize ourselves, to become our
potential . . . to express and activate all the capacities of the
organism."[87]

And I get that, but destiny is not that clinical and it's
way deeper. Artists have tried to capture the wonder of it too.
The screen writer Eric Roth had Forrest Gump reflect on it. "I
don't know if we each have a destiny or if we're all just floating
around accidental, like on a breeze. But I . . . I think maybe it's
both happening at the same time."[88]

You see, the reason the word "destiny" is so provocative
and personally evocative—why it inspires and frustrates—
is because it was hardwired into you before you even had a
body that would identify you. And until you find it, until you
discover your destiny, you will scratch it like an itch. And

daydream. And get frustrated. And maybe have a mid-life crisis. For sure, you'll cry.

Blame God. Seriously, it's his fault.

Before you were born, God created you with all your uniqueness and quirks and gifts and personality to do a thing. To fulfill a particular destiny.

Here it is: "For we are God's masterpiece, created in Christ Jesus to do good works, which God prepared in advance for us to do." (Ephesians 2:10)

Let's break that down a bit.

You are God's masterpiece. He not only loves you but he likes you. Before you were even born he stepped back and said, "I am quite fond of that one! I love everything about her. I love everything about him. There is no one like her in this world. He is one of a kind. Wow!" Masterpiece.

You were created to do good works. This is your destiny. This is that thing that makes your soul itch 'til you find it. It's like he embedded a homing device in your heart that will guide you to your peculiar contribution to the world. But what are "good works"? They are the kind of actions that God himself would define as good. And by now you know what I believe God would say are good works: they are the actions that heal the 6 Broken Places of the world. You were created to heal the SEPARATION of mankind from God and/or the PAIN that human beings experience and/or the ISOLATION that we feel from others and/or the interpersonal and interracial HATRED of humankind and/or the DECAY of the creation and/or the vast systems of INJUSTICE in our world.

You were created to be a NURTURER, an ACTIVIST, an AMBASSADOR, a STEWARD, a HEALER, or a CHAMPION. Which will it be? He prepared you "in advance" to be this. As in waaaaay back before you were born.

But, what of that phrase "in Christ Jesus"? This is key. And, honestly, it might be a stretch for those of you who are religiously agnostic. Regardless of how you feel about Jesus, nothing changes the fact that you were created with a God-given destiny. But, it's in being a Christ-follower that your destiny gets supercharged. To follow Christ is to be reunited with God your Father—the destiny giver. To follow Jesus is to be forgiven and set free from the weight of guilt. And to follow him is to be filled with his Spirit who empowers you to do your thing in this world. Your destiny in Jesus is a big deal. And amazingly, Jesus himself predicted that to follow him is to be able to do greater things than he ever did! What?

> "I tell you the truth, anyone who believes in me will do the same works I have done, and even greater works, because I am going to be with the Father." (John 14:12)

So, there it is. Your destiny awaits. You have a why to live for!

Now, how do you find it?

In the rest of this chapter I am going to introduce you to a concept or way of exploring your destiny. I call it "The Calling Quilt." It is a unique way of laying out before you pretty much all of your life. You'll be able to sit back and process the events that have shaped you, the experiences that have molded you, the pain that has defined you, the personality God gave you, the people who have inspired you, the passions that enflame you, and the broken places that infuriate you.

And, if you're patient and pay attention to what you see and think and feel as you construct your Calling Quilt, your calling will start to emerge, which will eventually give rise to your destiny.

First this caveat: This process is best done with the help of a wise friend, mentor, or even a counselor who can ask you good questions along the way and point out things you might overlook. I've walked many people through it and have celebrated with them the wide-eyed wonder of seeing a calling emerge out of their quilt. But, that said, it's not impossible to do this on your own. Take it slowly. Pray for discernment. Take good notes. Be honest. Watch what arises. And then, experiment. Do. Try. Dip your toe in the water of calling and get excited!

Now, let's clarify a few terms that get confused along the way.

Job – Your job is the work you do for which you are paid. It is your employment. Your job puts bread on the table. It is your occupation. It is your livelihood. A job is not your calling; but, for the truly blessed, sometimes it can be an outgrowth *of* your calling. To get paid to do the thing you were created by God for is outrageously wonderful. But, neither is it necessary. Your job can also simply be a support for your calling. And that's fine!

Career or vocation – The progression or series of jobs that start to form the long-term direction of your occupation is your career or vocation. A career forms over time as you leverage your education, your skill, and your experience. Your career may not be your calling. I've counselled many folks who, even after decades of work, still have the itch—still haven't found what they are looking for: their calling or destiny. But, then again, your career certainly could contain your calling. If that's the case, hallelujah! You hit it rich!

Role – Your role is the part you play in another person's life. You have all been playing some particular relational roles in your lives to date—son, daughter, friend, brother, sister, husband, wife, etc. And, of course, it goes without saying that those roles are crucial to you and those you love through them. But, if your life calling revolves around any of those roles, then I'm sorry, but that is too small a vision. Yes, I know God gives a lot of attention to helping us be better spouses, parents, and friends. But, what becomes of you when your children grow older, graduate, and move on, and suddenly you are faced with a new emptiness that is more than a vacant bedroom? Or what happens if your spouse precedes you to Heaven? Is your calling over? Again, your destiny might indeed wrap around the roles in your life, which would be spectacular; but, then again, it may not. Your roles in life are too small a vision to define your destiny.

> "Your profession is not what brings home your weekly paycheck, your profession is what you're put here on earth to do, with such passion and such intensity that it becomes spiritual in calling."
>
> – Vincent van Gogh

Calling - A calling is an invitation, a summons, or a beckoning. More specifically, the kind of calling I am talking about is the call of God. It is his invitation to purpose. It is his summons to you to meaning. It is his beckoning to you to change the world. Your calling is your why to live for. A calling can certainly envelop your job, your career, and your roles, or it may also be distinct. Your calling is uniquely yours. It's specific. And when you engage your calling you will find yourself smack-dab in the middle of a broken place, bringing healing and hope. Callings shift and morph over time as you move into the world with purpose. They usually build upon each other, moving surely toward their ultimate expression: your destiny.

> "I believe there's a calling for all of us. I know that every human being has value and purpose. The real work of our lives is to become aware. And awakened. To answer the call."
>
> – Oprah Winfrey

Destiny – Your destiny is your final calling or your calling fully realized. Destiny is your calling on steroids. It is the most poignant and powerful expression of your calling. Because destiny is discovered through iterations of calling, it usually doesn't emerge until later in life, after decades of experimentation and growth in your calling. Destiny is the ultimate why to live for, the culmination of a life of world changing!

Legacy – Legacy is that which you leave behind after a lifetime of work, career, roles, calling, and destiny. Legacy is that which will outlive you. Legacy will be seen most in the lives of people you have marked or impacted. Legacy will also be measured in the healing you have brought to one or more of the broken places. For some of you ambassadors, your legacy will be in the lives of people who have found God through you. For you healers, your legacy will be felt in the diminishment of pain. You champions will leave a legacy of some portion of a grave injustice being made right. The legacy you stewards leave will be seen in a portion of creation being restored to its God-desired wonder. The legacy of you

> "I think it would be well, and proper, and obedient, and pure, to grasp your one necessity and not let it go, to dangle from it limp wherever it takes you."
>
> – Annie Dillard

activists will be felt as peace replaces hate in your community. And you nurturers, your legacy will be in the many new relationships entered into with formerly lonely people. You won't be alive on Earth to enjoy the fruit of your destiny, but rest assured that all of Heaven will applaud your lifetime of investment in healing the broken places of the world.

> "Here's the choice that our Father wants us to understand as Christians: Do we want to be brave or safe? We simply can't be both. Doing God's will in a fallen world is inherently dangerous. In fact, if following Jesus does not feel dangerous, we should probably pause and check to see if it is Jesus we're following."

> – Gary Haugen, International Justice Mission

So then, how does a person go about discovering their calling and ultimately their destiny?

In short, you must become a student of you. You must do a deep dive into your life. You must analyze your makeup, your personalities, your gifts and skills, your experiences, your education, and your passions. And you must have a clear-eyed view of the highs and lows of your life, for in our brokenness, not just our victories, many callings are born.

David Brooks says in his book, *The Road to Character*, "Your ability to discern your vocation depends on the condition of your eyes and ears. Whether they are sensitive enough to understand the assignment your context is giving you."[89]

The best way to study your own life is to construct a calling quilt.

Quilts can be quite functional as a blanket or comforter. They can also be works of art. And many times, they are keepsakes that tell a story. Quilts normally are two layers of fabric with some substance such as wool or down between the layers stitched in patterns.

For our purposes I'd like you to imagine a T-shirt quilt. My daughter has one that she made after college. Each patch or segment of the quilt came from T-shirts she wore through her life to that point. It covered everything from elementary school through college—shows she was in, awards, sorority activities, etc. Though it wasn't a work of art (sorry, honey!), it was a labor of love and a cool history of her life. It tells a significant part of her story.

Now, instead of T-shirts, we're going to use stories and snippets from your life and lay them side by side in a quilt pattern. Take a piece of paper and draw lines on it that look like this:

In each one of those segments you are going to write something about you. Each segment will contain a small piece of your story from several different categories of your life: experiences, achievements, losses, joys, influences, jobs, personality traits, and much more.

On their own, each segment, story, experience, skill, or personality piece says something about you, but, stepping back, looking at the whole and connecting the dots, so to speak, this quilt can reveal your calling.

The individual pieces of your calling quilt come from the following categories. In just a few words each, place the answers to these questions, each in a separate section of the quilt. (See the sample.)

1. Education/ work / career
    a. What jobs have you had?
    b. Did you have a college major? Post-Grad?
    c. What were your fields of study?
    d. What has been your career?
2. Life experiences
    a. What are your powerful life-shaping high moments?
    b. What are your powerful life-shaping low moments?
    c. Who has influenced you most positively?
    d. Who has shaped you most negatively?
    e. What have been your "Aha" moments— surprises, inspirations, revelations?
3. Personality
    a. What are your Enneagram (or other personality test) results?
    b. What are your spiritual gifts?
4. What are your skills?
5. What are your hobbies and interests?
6. What are your passions?
    a. Which broken place concerns you the most? SEPARATION, PAIN, ISOLATION, DECAY,

HATRED, INJUSTICE?
b. What breaks your heart about the world?
c. What makes you mad about the world?
d. What experiences have you had in any of the broken places?
e. What have you read or watched that touched you deeply regarding the broken places?

Once you've filled a good part of your quilt start to look for connections. Begin to notice recurring themes. Note that sometimes obstacles and losses stimulate your life objectives. See how you have begun to take on the passions of the people in your life who've mentored you. Meld your personality with your gifts and your passions, and what have you got?

Then, find a trusted friend or ally and walk through your findings with them. Does your friend concur with your findings?

Finally, if you have a nudging from your calling quilt that may point to a direction, go there! Try it out! Give it a shot! Find a way to experiment with serving inside what looks like your calling and gauge the response.

Here's a hypothetical situation that I've made up of a woman I'll call Jennifer. Let's say Jennifer came to me and said she's burned out in her job as a social worker in the State Department of Child Services. She says, "There has to be something more." During an interview with her, coupled with some advance work on personality tests and some soul searching of her life, here is the quilt we constructed:

Working as a social worker in State Dept of Child Services	Took 2 mission trips to Ukraine to work with disabled orphans.	Had a powerful conversion experience on a wilderness trip.	Helped her mom raise her 3 younger siblings
Raised herself as her mother struggled with depression.	Lost father to cancer when she was 10.	Worked briefly as an adolescent counselor in a non-profit	Worked various jobs in urban area near her school
Introvert who is renewed by being in nature	Broken places that she cares about = Decay of the planet and pain of people	MA in social work	Grandpa who was a farmer that nurtured her. Time on the farm was her highlight
Spiritual gifts in mercy and helps	Enneagram 4	Loves animals	Vegan

That one is fairly obvious. It appears to me that Jennifer would be most fulfilled paring her love of animals and the outdoors with her passion to bring healing to struggling kids. Also, the early obstacles and tragedies of her life shaped her worldview and ability to relate to broken kids. And her education gave her a good base from which to work. Might her calling be on a rescue animal farm for disabled kids? A comfort animal program for foster kids?

So, what do you think? I know you are intrigued by it all. I've never met anyone who *isn't* dying to discover their why to live for because, of course, you are a masterpiece. Yeah, you know that by now.

Give it a try. Call up your friend. Print out a blank calling quilt, and one for them. Brew some coffee. Start thinking and praying and writing and discussing. And get ready to discover your destiny!

- Are you a NURTURER bringing love to the broken place of ISOLATION?

- Are you a HEALER offering comfort in the broken place of PAIN?

- Are you a STEWARD caring for God's creation that suffers under the broken place of DECAY?

- Are you a CHAMPION engaging the broken place of INJUSTICE?

- Are you an ACTIVIST fighting against the broken place of HATRED?

- Or are you an AMBASSADOR representing God in the broken place of SEPARATION?

What, my friend, is your why to live for? Where will your destiny intersect with our groaning world? And what are you waiting for?

AFTERWORD

I will not die an unlived life.
I will not live in fear
of falling or catching fire.
I choose to inhabit my days,
to allow my living to open me,
to make me less afraid,
more accessible,
to loosen my heart
until it becomes a wing,
a torch, a promise.
I choose to risk my significance,
to live so that which came to me as seed
goes to the next as blossom,
goes on as fruit. [90]

Dawna Markova
From *I Will Not Die an Unlived Life.*

ABOUT DAVE RODRIGUEZ

Dave Rodriguez is the founding and senior pastor of Grace Church in Noblesville, IN. For the past twenty-seven years, Dave has led Grace to advance the Kingdom of God in central Indiana and around the world. He has served the local church in pastoral ministry for over forty years.

Grace Church has planted six churches in the United States, along with churches in London, England and Sydney, Australia. Grace currently worships in three campuses in central Indiana. In addition, Grace operates a Care Center that meets the needs of over 500 families a week through a choice food pantry, referral services, ESL classes, micro-loans, and a car care ministry.

Dave's education began at the University of Pittsburgh. He went on to graduate with both his undergraduate and graduate degrees from Moody Bible Institute in Chicago. He also received an honorary doctorate from Taylor University.

Dave has been happily married to Penny for nearly forty years. They have two grown children, Barry Rodriguez (married to Olivia) and Lucy King (married to Kevin). When not living out his calling in ministry, you'll likely find Dave slaving over a hot stove working on the hobby he loves—being an amateur chef.

NOTES

1.   *Willard, Dallas, Divine Conspiracy, New York:HarperCollins, 1998, pp. 25-26.*
2.   *Guder, Daryl, editor, The Missional Church, Grand Rapids, MI: Wm. Be Eerdmans Publishing Co., 1998, p. 91.*
3.   *McLaren, Brian, The Secret Message of Jesus, Nashville, TN: Thomas Nelson, 2005, p.31.*
4.   *Kraybill, Donald, The Upside Down Kingdom, Scottdale, PA: Herald Press, 1978,1990, p. 19.*
5.   *Wright, NT, Surprised by Hope, New York: Harper Collins, 2008. p.201.*
6.   *Wright, Christopher J.H., The Mission of God, IL: Intervarsity Press, 2006, p.309.*
7.   *Wright, NT, Surprised by Hope, p.208.*
8.   *Haugen, Gary, Just Courage, 2008, Downers Grove, IL: Intervarsity Press, page 113.*
9.   *Rodriguez, Barry, Into the World Next Door, self-published, 2018, pg 26.*
10.   *Fosdick, Harry Emerson. The Meaning of Prayer, Association Press, New York, 1915, p.101.*
11.   *ibid, p. 12*
12.   *Haugen, Gary, Good News about Injustice, Downers Grove, IL: InterVarsity Press, 1999, p 37.*
13.   *https://thefatherlessgeneration.wordpress.com/*
14.   *https://www.cigna.com/newsroom/news-releases/2018/new-cigna-study-reveals-lonliness-at-epidemic-levels-in-america*
15.   *Winner, Lauren, Girl meets God, Chapel Hill, NC: Algonquin Books, 2002, p. 94.*
16.   *Gerst-Emerson, Kerstin, PhD and Jayani Jayawardhana, PhD, "Loneliness as a Public Health Issue: The Impact of*

Loneliness on Health Care Utilization Among Older Adults," Am J Public Health, May 2015, 105(5): 1013–1019, https://www.ncbi.nlm.nih.gov/pmc/articles/PMC4386514/?report=classic

17. Pressman SD, Cohen S, Miller GE, Barkin A, Rabin BS, Treanor JJ. "Loneliness, social network size, and immune response to influenza vaccination in college freshmen." Department of Psychology, Carnegie Mellon University, Pittsburgh, PA, Health Psychology, American Psychological Association 2005, Vol. 24 https://pdfs.semanticscholar.org/eaad/ba889b70ed8275cc844e6de7edd241e26116.pdf

18. UCLA genomics researcher Steve Cole explained to NPR in 2015

19. Fetters, Ashley, "What Loneliness Does to the Human Body," The Cut-Science of US, https://www.thecut.com/2018/01/the-health-effects-of-loneliness.html, Jan. 22, 2018.

20. Brigham Young University, "Loneliness Might Be A Bigger Health Risk Than Smoking Or Obesity," https://www.forbes.com/sites/quora/2017/01/18/loneliness-might-be-a-bigger-health-risk-than-smoking-or-obesity/#30d23cd425d1, Jan 18, 2017.

21. Olds, Jacqueline, M.D. and Richard Schwartz, M.D., The Lonely American: Drifting Apart in the Twenty-first Century, Beacon Press, Boston, MA, 2009.

22. ibid, p. 6

23. Winch, Guy, PhD. "The Unexpected Loneliness of Combat Vets and POWs with PTSD, The loneliness of returning home after trauma" Psychology Today, Jun 04, 2014.

24. Nouwen, Henri, http://www.goodreads.com/author/show/4837.Henri_J_M_Nouwen

25. Peterson, Eugene, The Pastor: A Memoir, New York: Harper Collins, 2011, p 195.

26. Meyer, Danny, Setting the Table, New York: Harper Collins, 2006, p.65-66.

27.   McKeown, Greg, *Essentialism, The Disciplined Pursuit of Less*, New York: Crown Publishing, p. 5

28.   Fosdick, p .101

29.   ibid, p.19

30.   McKeown, p. 7

31.   ibid, p. 13

32.   ibid, p. 15

33.   Meyer, p. 251

34.   ibid

35.   Denizet-Lewis, Benoit, "Why are more American Teenagers than ever Suffering From Severe anxiety?" *New York Times Magazine*, Oct. 11, 2017.

36.   https://www.nimh.nih.gov/health/statistics/major-depression.shtml

37.   https://www.psychologytoday.com/us/blog/anxiety-files/200804/how-big-problem-is-anxiety

38.   Sheridan, Jill, "Fishers Takes On Mental Health Stigma" Indiana Public Media.org, https://indianapublicmedia.org/news/fishers-takes-mental-health-stigma-100282/, Posted June 12, 2016.

39.   https://www.cdc.gov/drugoverdose/epidemic/index.html

40.   Stark, Rodney, *The Rise of Christianity: A Sociologist Reconsiders History*, Princeton, MA: University Press, Princeton, 1996 p. 82-83.

41.   https://www.samaritanspurse.org/article/as-new-film-debuts-march-30-dr-kent-brantly-continues-to-share-good-news/

42.   https://www.cbsnews.com/news/when-hospitals-become-targets-in-syria-civil-war-60-minutes/

43.   Gillis, Justin, "Climate Change is Complex. We've got answers to your questions," *New York Times*, https://www.nytimes.com/interactive/2017/climate/what-is-climate-change.html, Nov. 2017

44. https://blog.franciscanmedia.org/franciscan-spirit/saint-francis-of-assisi-and-the-animals

45. https://www.adventure-journal.com/2013/10/the-aj-list-20-inspiring-quotes-from-john-muir/

46. https://vault.sierraclub.org/john_muir_exhibit/about/

47. https://www.huffingtonpost.com/2015/04/22/nature-prayers-earth-day_n_7112274.html

48. ibid

49. http://www.beliefnet.com/prayers/protestant/gratitude/thank-you-for-this-earth.aspx

50. http://acen.anglicancommunion.org/media/61546/Stewardship-of-Creation-prayer.pdf

51. https://www.unilever.com/sustainable-living/

52. http://www.wm.com/thinkgreen/index.jsp

53. https://www.patagonia.com/worn-wear.html

54. Sermon delivered by Tim Ayers on July 24, 2005 at Grace Church, Noblesville, IN

55. http://www.sbc.net/resolutions/year/2017

56. Yankahnov, Ekow N., "Can My Children Be Friends With White People?," New York Times: Nov. 11, 2017

57. http://faithfullymagazine.com/talking-racial-reconciliation-white-supremacy/

58. https://www.christianitytoday.com/history/2018/june/nick-chiles-early-anti-racism-activist-history-forgot.html

59. http://www.christianitytoday.com/ct/2017/august-web-only/christians-combat-racism-theologically-charlottesville.html

60. ibid

61. https://alarm-inc.org/rwanda/

62. https://www.naim.ca/

63. Holloway, Kali, "11 Things White People Can Do to Be Real Anti-Racist Allies: Here's what it means to do the challenging work of fighting white supremacy," AlterNet April 27, 2015

64.   Raybon, Patricia, "The Dead White Man Who Could Fix Our Race Problem: Oswald Chambers," Christianity Today, https://www.christianitytoday.com/women/2017/november/ dead-white-man-fix-our-race-problem-oswald-chambers.html, November 21, 2017

65.   Sahim, "11 Things . . .," ibid

66.   Wang, "11 Things . . .," ibid

67.   from @samsanders Twitter thread, https://twitter.com/ samsanders, August 12, 2017.

68.   Brown, "11 Things . . .," ibid

69.   Willard, Divine Conspiracy

70.   Pavlovitz, John, "The Christian Myth of America's Moral Decay," HuffPost, https://www.huffingtonpost.com/ john-pavlovitz/the-christian-myth-of-americas-moral-decay_b_10022720.html, updated May 19, 2017

71.   Lewis, Charles, "Truth and Lies in the Trump Era," The Nation.com, October 2017

72.   ibid

73.   Friedman, Edwin, A Failure of Nerve, Church Publishing, Inc.,1999, 2007

74.   Zacharias, Ravi, Can Man Live Without God, Nashville, TN: W Publishing Group, Thomas Nelson, 1994

75.   ibid

76.   https://billygraham.org/answer/billy-grahams-final-answer-wanted-remembered/

77.   Everts, Don and Doug Schaupp, I Once Was Lost, Downers Grove, IL: IVP Books, 2008, p. 19.

78.   White, James Emery, Meet Generation Z, Grand Rapids, MI: Baker Books, 2017, p. 18.

79.   ibid

80.   Henderson, Jim, Evangelism Without Additives, Colorado Springs, CO: WaterBrook Press, 2005, p. 11.

81.   Ibid

82.   *Everts and Schaupp, ibid, p. 34-35.*

83.   *ibid, p. 57.*

84.   *ibid*

85.   *Henderson, ibid, p. from the foreword, p. x*

86.   *Mattson, Rick, Faith is Like Skydiving, Downers Grove, IL: Intervarsity Press 2014, p. 190.*

87.   *Rogers, Carl, On Becoming a Person, New York: Houghton Mifflin, 1961, p. 350-1.*

88.   *Zemeckis, Robert, dir., Forrest Gump, Paramount Pictures, 1994.*

89.   *Brooks, David, The Road to Character, New York: Random House, 2015, pg. 24.*

90.   *Markova, Donna, I Will Not Die an Unlived Life: Reclaiming Purpose and Passion, San Francisco: Conari Press, 2000, pg. 1.*